WE
STILL
LOVE
YOU

BOB

First Church of the Brethren
1340 Forge Road
Carlisle, Pennsylvania 17013

WE
STILL
LOVE
YOU

BOB

A mother's struggle with a problem child

Dorothea Marvin Nyberg

Foreword by Anne Ortlund

Revised Edition

BRETHREN PRESS
Elgin, Illinois

We Still Love You, Bob

Brethren Press, 1451 Dundee Avenue, Elgin, IL 60120

Cover design by Kathy Kline

Edited by Leslie R. Keylock

Library of Congress Cataloging in Publication Data

Nyberg, Dorothea M. (Dorothea Marvin), 1923-
    We still love you, Bob

    Reprint. Originally published: Chappaqua, N.Y.: Christian
Herald Books, c 1979.
    1. Child psychopathology—United States—Biography.
2. Nyberg, Bob. I. Title.
RJ499.N89 1984   362.2'092'4 [B]   84-18593
ISBN 0-87178-925-6

Printed in the United States of America

Dedication

To my friends Karen Ann Wojahn and Sheila Cragg whose prayers, encouragement, and editorial advice kept me working toward the finished manuscript.

Plaudits also to family and friends who were supportive with their love and prayers during our "trying" times.

Finally, special recognition and thanks to God for his forgiveness when we erred and the strength that was only available through his caring love.

Contents

Foreword

Having an adopted child of my own, I read Dorothea Nyberg's story of her adopting her "charmer" with special interest. Which becomes the overruling factor in an adopted child's development—heredity or environment?

In the case of our Nels, I think environment. He couldn't be more *ours*. As he himself wrote when he was fifteen in my book *Children Are Wet Cement* (Flemming H. Revell, 1981)

> My parents have "cemented" me into their ways and beliefs. I don't always agree with them, but I don't think we would have a normal family if everything was perfect. When it comes right down to it, I will always be 100 percent behind my folks, and I'm sure my brother and sisters would agree with me.
>
> . . . I think of some of the things where certain impressions of them can be seen in me or my brother or sisters. . . .
>
> I love my folks and always will, but really I have no choice because part of me is them, and I like myself, so that automatically says I like them too. The End."

On the other hand, heredity and the environment of the first year, according to Dorothea's assessment in her final chapter, seemed too powerful a force to be overcome in the raising of her adopted son, "the charmer."

Parents suffering through "the difficult years" will appreciate Dorothea's strong faith in God, her patience, her ability to cope. Deftly described, each incident in the handling of this "impossible" child may give the readers some insight into handling their own.

May God bless the use of this skillfully and sensitively written book.

Anne Ortlund
Newport Beach
California

Prologue

This book is being written for the hundreds of families who have problem Bobs, Joes, Marys, Sues—families torn apart, hurting, desperate, feeling unable to take any more from their "lost" young people.

As I relived our story, I could see how God used Bob to train us in total submission to him. God had the answers, God knew the reasons, while we groaned under the questions that bombarded our minds.

It is a constant struggle to be patient, to be loving, and to remain filled with the Holy Spirit. Without these strengths, Don and I could not have survived.

There is only one answer for Bob and for parents . . . the Lord Jesus Christ. He promised his Comforter. Life is not easy, especially with a troubled child, but God never promised it would be easy. The Israelites, God's chosen people, spent four hundred years in bondage in Egypt, then forty more years in the wilderness preparing themselves for the Promised Land. How they suffered!

Throughout history it seems that the "saints" suffer most deeply. It was through suffering that their commitment to Jesus became complete. It has been that way for Don and me, too. We also learned the necessity of total relinquishment.

Jesus, the only perfect man ever created, has known our

deep despair. He knows how hard it is for Bob to make right choices because he, who never sinned, was tempted by the master tempter. He knows suffering because he suffered the most agonizing death ever devised. And the miraculous part is that through his suffering *we* became blessed with eternal life. He will be our strength forever.

Our children are only on "loan" to us from God. If he chooses to allow us to suffer through the actions of these gifts, we can grow closer to him through the pain.

Don and I know that no matter how far or how fast Bob runs, God is with him. God loves and forgives. When Bob tires of running (and he's slowing down), perhaps he will invite Jesus into his life and give himself totally to Jesus. Then the waiting and suffering will not have been in vain. God has unlimited patience. We, as parents, need the same, and it can only come from him.

1
An Additional Twig

My hand shook as I replaced the telephone receiver. My heart pounded wildly and nausea gripped my stomach. I stood at the window and watched Bob stride across the golf course, his defiant steps taking him toward the highway. *What kind of a mother am I to turn my own son in to the police?*

This child we longed for filled our days with happiness, joy, and laughter. Yet there were other periods to remember —times of sadness, tears, despair. Bob made our lives a mixture of these ingredients.

After five years of marriage, God blessed us with a beautiful son we named David. He was the first grandchild for my parents and the first grandson for my husband's family. The only sadness in our lives was that no brother or sister appeared during the two years following David's arrival. We didn't want David to be an only child, so we discussed adoption with Dr. Decker, our family doctor.

"Go ahead if you want more than two kids," he told us. "But I'll bet as soon as you adopt you'll get pregnant."

We started the long and rigorous adoption procedure, much more difficult than the labor pains of birth. We were afraid we wouldn't be accepted because we already had David and we had no medical proof of my inability to conceive. On the other hand, I did have the RH negative factor that might be a plus for adoption.

We applied through our state agency. The home study went smoothly. We had a secure marriage and a stable family background. When the social worker asked, "What age child do you prefer?" Don facetiously answered, "Oh, a girl about eighteen should do!"

I thought, *Now he's done it—that crazy sense of humor.* But the worker only laughed and continued.

"I prefer a brand new baby right from delivery," I specified.

Don added, "Up to three years of age."

"Boy or girl?"

"Either sex is acceptable," we both answered together. "We left it up to God with David and we'll leave it to him again."

Several months later we received official notification that we had been approved for child placement. Now the real waiting began!

Months passed. Each day I prayed that this might be *the day.* "I want a child close enough to David to be a real pal. Why is this taking so long?" I questioned Don.

"Perhaps this is a lesson in patience for us both," he responded.

David, too, was looking forward to welcoming a new brother or sister. But our wait continued.

Finally one afternoon an official-looking brown envelope arrived with the rest of our mail.

"Don! Don!" I shouted into the phone moments later, still out of breath from my dash from the mailbox. "A letter from the adoption agency! Listen! *'We have a one-year-old boy, named Bobby, that we feel will fit into your home. He is tiny for his age but mentally alert, inquisitive, and adorable. We will bring him to your city and place him in a boarding home if you are interested in meeting him.'"*

"Wow! A one-year-old would be perfect!" exclaimed Don. "David turned three last month. That would make them just two years apart."

"Exactly the spacing we hoped for," I added.

"This must be the child that God has chosen for us," Don enthused.

"I think it would be upsetting for Bobby to be moved to a new boarding home here. Can you arrange a day off so we can go up there to see him?"

"Sure."

We made plans to see Bobby the following day. Leaving early, we arrived ahead of our scheduled appointment. We were so anxious to meet this longed-for child!

"What information is available about Bobby's background?" I asked the social worker after we were ushered into her office.

"We're not allowed to give out too much information," she replied, "but there are some areas I can cover. Ask me questions, and I'll try to answer them. We want to talk about his background. If there are any gray areas, we want them to be covered before we allow you to see the child."

"Are his parents alive?" Don asked.

"Yes. Bobby's mother left him at the hospital when he was born without even seeing him."

"It's hard for me to imagine any mother not wanting to see her child," I replied.

"It's often easier for them that way. Bobby's parents married very young and had four children in as many years. I presume she could not face the thought of caring for another baby. They have been a welfare family."

"He's almost a year old now," Don stated. "What has happened to him since he was born?"

"Bobby's father took him home to his two older brothers and attempted to care for all three children. His mother had taken the oldest, a girl, and disappeared."

"And now Bobby's father wants to give him up?" Don asked.

"All three boys were made wards of the state when Bobby was six months old. The two older boys have been placed in permanent homes. Bobby has been in a foster home recovering from hernia surgery and waiting for placement."

"What about his father?" we both asked.

"He wasn't able to care for them properly, and he felt that it would be best for the children to be placed for adoption," the social worker explained. "Bobby's father has been unable to find his niche in the working world, but he is a handsome man, a real 'charmer.'"

"Charmer, charmer." How that word was to haunt me. It is frightening to realize how large a part heredity plays in a person's life. The social worker's description mirrors Bob precisely, and yet he has never been told these facts about his father.

Bobby was asleep when we arrived at the foster home. The foster mother gave us more information while we waited for Bobby to wake up. "When Bobby came to us, he was pitiful—simply filthy. I cut the clothes from his little, malnourished body. He had, no doubt, cried by the hour, because he had a hernia. Welfare paid for his hospitalization and surgical repair. Now he is starting to fill out. We love him. He has become happy and content in our home."

Soon we heard sounds of stirring in the upstairs bedroom. We will never forget our first glimpse of Bobby as he was carried down the stairs. The back of his beautifully shaped head was full of gleaming golden curls, damp with the perspiration of sleep. As he turned, he stretched, yawned, and opened his vivid blue eyes to scrutinize us. He then broke into a friendly electrical grin that illuminated his face with the mischief inherent in his personality. He was the stereotyped, adorably beautiful, golden-haired baby about whom all adoptive parents dream. Bobby won our hearts instantly. Diminutive for his age, he had a delicate, fragile look. With his golden curls and impish, smiling blue eyes, he was indeed a "charmer."

The social worker said, "Why don't you two take a ride around the block and discuss your feelings about Bobby?"

Don spoke up without even needing to look at me for a sign. "There is no necessity for us to do that. We want him!" I concurred completely. We bundled Bobby into David's old snowsuit, got into the car, and headed home with our new son.

2
Nightmare Nights

It was a long, quiet, trip. I can still feel Bobby's blue eyes gazing earnestly into mine. I wondered what thoughts were wending their way through his little mind. He spoke very few words and, as I chatted with him and with Don, his eyes never wavered from my face. Finally he fell asleep, and I felt him relax for the first time.

When we arrived home, my parents and David were there waiting. I gently awakened Bobby. "This is your new home," I said. "We are going in to meet your new brother and your grandparents. Your brother's name is David."

Bobby clung tightly to me and didn't utter a sound. When we entered the house, David ran up to Bobby, shouting, "Hi, Bobby! Are you my new brother?" Bobby maintained his silence, staring at all the people in the room. We realized that it was too much for him to comprehend.

Mom said, "Come on, David, help me get dinner ready." She took him by the hand, and they quietly moved into the kitchen. Don and Dad followed her lead and headed for the dining room to play cribbage.

Bobby looked around and, seeing no more strangers, decided to get down from my lap and do a bit of exploring. He walked over to a building that David had built with his blocks and knocked it down. But when Dad came back into the room,

Bobby crawled behind the drapes to hide.

We all tried to be casual and act as though Bobby had always been a part of the family. Supper was soon ready, and Bobby sat in the highchair and wolfed down his dinner. He had an insatiable appetite that remained through the years. Bobby still needed the comfort and security of a bedtime bottle. I warmed some milk and tucked him into his crib with his bottle. That first night he went to sleep without any problem.

Each day Bobby became more secure. He definitely felt safer with Mom or me. It was a long time before Don or Dad could pick him up to love him and be certain he wouldn't start to scream. Because I was with him all day—feeding him, attending to his needs—he *had* to trust me.

Our little Bobby had moved from a father who may have abused him, and certainly neglected him, to a hospital for surgery, and then to a new, temporary home. There, after being loved and adored by his foster parents, he allowed himself to reciprocate their love. But suddenly he found himself abruptly taken away by complete strangers. No wonder he was bewildered!

Because I gave so much of my time to Bobby, David, naturally, became jealous of his new little brother. "How would you like to go and spend tonight and Saturday with Grandma and Grandpa?" I suggested.

"Can I go right now?" he replied.

A telephone call to Mom verified her availability, and we packed David up and drove him to his grandparents' home. *It will be good for Bobby to have a day alone with just Don and me*, I thought.

Early the next morning the telephone rang. It was David. "Mommy, I want to come home."

Put Grandma on the phone, please."

When Mom came, I heard her send David to another room for something, and then she said, "He was up early, wanting to go home. When I asked why, he replied, 'I want to go home and hit Bobby!'"

Don and I were relieved that David's jealousy was coming

out in a normal manner, rather than being held inside. We were also glad he was a sound sleeper, because what Bobby put us through could have been traumatic for David.

We called them nightmare nights. We would tuck the two boys into their beds after hearing them say their prayers and give Bobby his bottle. Then peace reigned—sometimes. But, in the middle of the night Bobby started to scream. We got up, changed his diaper, gave him another bottle, and put him back to bed. But no matter what we did, he continued to scream.

We tried feeding him his favorite foods (he was always hungry during the day), but to no avail. If we took him into bed with us, he screamed louder. I walked the floor with him; he still screamed. If Don tried to pacify him, the screaming became worse. After several nights of this, I called Dr. Decker, who felt it was an adjustment period for Bobby and that he'd soon stop. The screaming continued, however, until Don and I were both exhausted. For close to three months, Bobby disrupted our sleep several times a week.

We didn't want to rush Bobby to the doctor, forcing him to cope with one more stranger. Now we felt we must. The lack of sleep was wearing my disposition thin. I phoned the doctor. "Bring him in," he said.

"He is physically perfect, small for his age," Dr. Decker reported, "but with his appetite he will grow. I'll give you a prescription for elixir of phenobarbital. Give him a teaspoonful if he wakes up and begins to scream at night. This is a mild amount."

Two nights later, we had another episode. With the first wail, Don said, "Try that medicine and see if it works, I'm too tired to stay awake all night again." After changing his diaper, we administered a spoonful of medicine. Bobby whimpered a little but soon settled down and slept soundly the rest of the night.

Exactly one week passed, and again Bobby's wails shattered our sleep. "Give him more of that super juice," Don said. We repeated the previous week's routine, and Bobby snuggled down in his crib. I lay awake thinking about that miracle elixir and how well it worked. After a time I became aware of Bobby's restless movements. I tiptoed into his room and discovered him rooting around in his crib with what appeared to be big bites on his body. I took him out of the crib to see if a spider or some kind of bug might be in the bed. Nothing was in sight, so I hugged him and tucked him back into the crib and wondered, *What are those marks? Were we getting measles in the family?* I fell asleep with thoughts whirling in my mind.

The next day was Sunday. I slipped into Bobby's room to see how he looked. I was horrified! I ran to the telephone and called Dr. Decker at home. "Bobby is covered with red welts," I said. "What could be the trouble?"

"Have you used the phenobarbital?" he asked.

"Yes. We gave him a teaspoonful last Saturday night, a week go, and he went right to sleep like a doll. Then last night he woke up again so we gave him another dose. It settled him down, but later he was restless and I noticed the bites."

"Those aren't bites," the doctor replied. "They are hives, no doubt a delayed reaction to the phenobarbital."

"Oh, no! What will the spoonful we gave him last night do?"

"He will get worse before he gets better." Dr. Decker said. "I'll call the drugstore and order a prescription for him as soon as it opens. We'll try to control the reaction orally."

We knew that there would be no Sunday school and church for us that Sunday. Don drove to the drugstore to greet the druggist at opening time to be there to ask a question when the doctor called. After Dr. Decker gave the prescription to the druggist, Don spoke to him. "Can Bobby burst or split his skin? He is swelling so badly that his eyes are almost closed and his ears look like red sails."

"No," the doctor replied, "but he'll be miserable. Use baking soda for the itch and keep him as comfortable as possible. I don't want to hospitalize him."

We gave Bobby benedryl all day, but the red welts continued to swell. They fused together until he resembled a red patent leather baby. Anticipating a bad night, we shipped

David off to his grandparents.

Since Bobby always slept well in the car, we spent the night alternately driving and holding our sleeping red baby. He was un unbelievable sight. His ears looked like Dumbo the elephant's ears. His eyes were swollen completely shut. He had no arch in his feet. They were swollen solidly flat and terribly red. His whole body was red, red, red!

The sun was just coming up when we called Dr. Decker again.

"Take him right to the hospital," he told us when we described Bobby. "We can't avoid it. Can you leave David someplace so you can stay with Bobby for the day?"

"Of course. David is at Mom and Dad's home now; he can stay there. We'll be at the hospital in a few minutes."

"I'll call and have them ready for him. We'll get faster action by giving him medication by injection."

As soon as we reached the hospital, Bobby was admitted. Every twenty minutes throughout the day a nurse appeared with the dreaded needle. At first Bobby took the shots without too much complaint, but each time a nurse walked by the door, he would get up on his knees and start to cry. He feared another needle. I would pick him up, love him, pat him, and he'd doze off to sleep again.

After work Don came in to relieve me. Bobby seemed glad to see him and cuddled with him the way he had been cuddling with me. By evening his back was one solid red hive, but his eyes, ears, and the rest of his body were nearly normal.

As we were about to leave for the night, a nurse stopped at the door to ask how Bobby was doing. The rustle of her starched uniform was enough of a signal to set Bobby off. Art cuddled our sobbing, wailing baby while I went to telephone Dr. Decker.

"Can we take him home?" I asked. "He is so frightened. My staying here with him at the hospital may have built some security for him. Now if we can take him home to his own bed, he may realize that he is to be ours forever and that there'll be no more changes in his life."

"All right," Dr. Decker replied, "but if you can't get him settled down by 10:00 P.M., call me back. We'll have to put him
back in the hospital and get this night problem solved."

We took Bobby home, put him in his crib, kissed him good
night, and that was the end of our nightmare nights. God, in his
infinite wisdom, had chosen that circumstance to set our little
one's mind at ease.

3
Double Blessing

"I can't understand why I'm so tired," I remarked to Don one Saturday morning. "I wish I could just stay in bed and sleep this whole day."

"Crawl back in. I'll chase the boys for a while. Maybe you should call Dr. Decker. You do look tired, and Bobby's been letting us sleep all night for more than a month."

I followed Don's advice and scheduled an appointment with Dr. Decker. But before the date of my appointment arrived, I realized the reason for my fatigue. *Dr. Decker will fall out his chair laughing,* I thought. *Just as he predicted, I'm probably pregnant. Now our family will be perfect. We'll have three kids at least, spaced two years apart. Isn't God wonderful!*

Dr. Decker's office was in the hospital, at the far end of the building and down a long hallway. Patients waiting to see various doctors sat on chairs along the hall. I took the boys with me. Bobby's adjustment to the family was progressing, and he was becoming friendly with strangers. As we walked down the hall to Dr. Decker's office, Bobby sauntered up to the waiting patients. If I didn't catch his hand, he slapped them. He did not hit hard; his touches were just friendly swats with a "Hi" attached.

Dr. Decker cheerfully confirmed my suspicions.

As the adoption proceedings moved toward their finalization, Mr. Smith, our social worker, paid us our first visit. He wanted to check on Bobby's adjustment to us and ours to him. To the boy's dismay we wore our Sunday clothes. We were ready to show Mr. Smith that we were a well-adjusted family. I hoped to hide my pregnant condition. We didn't want to chance its affecting the adoption procedures.

"Bobby, how do you like your new mommy and daddy and brother?" Mr. Smith asked.

Bobby just grinned and didn't waste any of his few words. David spoke up for him. "He likes us fine, and we like him, too. Now can we get into our play clothes and go outside?"

"Yes, scoot along," Don replied. "We just wanted Mr. Smith to see you clean and shiny."

After the boys escaped from the room, Mr. Smith turned to us. "How do you feel Bobby is adjusting to your home?"

"We had a rough time those first few months. Boy, those sleepless nights! But now Bobby's settled in. He still doesn't like to go to strange places," I explained, "but he's coming out of his shell."

"Yes, and now we're wondering if he isn't becoming too forward at times," Don laughingly interjected. In a more serious vein he continued, "He still seems uneasy when I try to pick him up to cuddle him. Sometimes he will accept my advances, and sometimes he won't."

"Bobby seems unsure of big men," I added. "He is much more comfortable with women."

"Has he been a discipline problem?" Mr. Smith asked.

"He has trouble accepting the 'nos' of life. We didn't move things out of David's reach, and we decided that Bobby, too, had to learn that there are certain forbidden objects in the house. When he reaches for a vase or a knickknack, we pick it up and let him see and examine it while we hold it. Then we explain that it is Mommy's or Daddy's and he must only look at it, that his toys are in the toy box. He doesn't like that rule, but he's learning."

Mr. Smith left a short while later, apparently satisfied that Bobby was adjusting to our family. As far as I could tell, he was unaware that I was pregnant.

We continued having problems in the 'no' area with Bobby. We often discovered him playing with a forbidden item. When we removed it, he displayed his displeasure with a screaming tantrum. However, screaming in the daytime was no trauma to our household. He'd soon tire and wander off to his own playthings.

As Bobby's first year with us was growing to a close, our attorney began drawing up the final adoption papers. Knowing that a court appearance was necessary to complete the adoption, I called Mr. Smith. "I wonder if it would be possible to speed up this procedure," I said. "I'm pregnant, and I don't want to be hospitalized on the day of our court appearance."

"When is the new baby due?" he asked, as if pregnancy were an everyday happening in adoptions.

"In March, so I hope that we can get everything finished in February."

"I'm sure we can arrange for Bobby to come in for some final testing, similar to the tests we gave David when you made application for adoption. We call it psychoanalysis. The tests make sure that Bobby is normal in all phases of his development. I'll call as soon as I can schedule the date."

When the day arrived, Bobby and I went to the psychologist's office alone. Her waiting room was pleasant. Toys and children's books were scattered here and there.

"I'm Mrs. Nyberg," I explained to the receptionist. She smiled and told me it would be a few minutes.

I sat in a large overstuffed chair leafing through a magazine. Bobby busied himself with some of the toys. A few moments later the door to the inner office opened. A smartly dressed woman with a friendly smile beckoned Bobby.

"Come in, Bobby," she smiled. "We'll play some games together."

Still somewhat skittish about new people and strange places, Bobby ran to me and crawled up on my lap (what there was of a lap at that stage of number three's development). I hugged him and said, "Hey, look at all those nice toys over there to play with? Wouldn't you like to see that big truck? I bet you could have fun with that one." Bobby soon became interested enough to slide off my lap and investigate the toy truck. I quietly explained to the psychologist the reasons for Bobby's reluctance. I described his difficult adjustment to our home and family.

"Bobby," she said again, after I had clarified his actions, "let's go into my office. Your mommy will come too."

"Okay," he replied, running ahead of us.

"Sit in the corner, Mrs. Nyberg, and please say nothing, even if he asks you a question. Just pretend you aren't here." I settled back in my chair, expecting to behold a stellar performance by our little clown. I knew his potential for an audience. He was that "charmer" when he wanted to be.

Bobby and the psychologist began the test by playing together, putting square blocks into square holes and round ones into round holes. Bobby breezed through that portion of the test without even glancing at me. Then the psychologist began giving instructions. "Take this pencil and put it on your chair. Then come back and get this one and take it to your mother."

Bobby took the first pencil and put in on his chair. Then he returned, picked up the second one and carried it to his chair. Still holding the second pencil, he hesitated, then turned to the psychologist. His expression was clearly a question.

"That's fine, Bobby," she said.

"You may color now for a while. Draw me a picture of you and your family." While Bobby was busy drawing, she quietly explained, "He did very well on that test. A child of two can't follow many directions in a row. I would not have been surprised if he quit after the first set, but he came back and got the second pencil. It was only the final instruction to take it to you that bogged him down. I really didn't expect him to get that far."

"It has been a fascinating session to observe," I replied, "and it convinces me that Bobby should be as sharp as Dave."

The final test centered around a group of cards. The psychologist showed Bobby a picture on the first card and asked, "What is this, Bobby?"

"Shoes," he promptly answered.

She then placed that card at the back of the pack and showed him the next card. This time the picture was of a tree. "What is this, Bobby?"

His impishness expanded as he felt more at ease. He tossed her a big grin, wrinkled his little nose at me and with a smirky smile, said in an important tone of voice, "Shoes!"

The psychologist went through the whole pack of cards and had a repeat performance with every item depicted—Bobby's impish grin at both of us and his loud declaration, "Shoes!"

When the testing was completed, the psychologist opened the door and said, "Bobby, run and play with the toys again while I talk to your mother." Bobby, who had been inactive too long, ran off in a hurry.

"Mrs. Nyberg," she said to me, "I have heard about children like Bobby, but I have never met one before. There is absolutely nothing wrong with his intelligence, but there are no results to this test. Because he didn't cooperate, I could no more give him a numerical rating than I could fly. He had me buffaloed, and *he* knew it!" Her statement would ring in my ears through later years during other episodes with Bobby. This ability mixed with his "charm" was rather frightening.

That evening I told Don about the tests. "What do you think about Bobby's abilities to baffle the experts and enchant other people? Could those qualities lead to his becoming a con artist as an adult?"

"Honey," Don replied, "he's just a mischievous little boy. Don't think about such things." The subject was dropped.

Later as I lay in bed, I talked with God about my feelings, asking him again to guide us with Bobby. It was becoming more difficult to leave Bobby and his problems in God's hands.

In the meantime we had been preparing the boys for the new brother or sister who would soon be arriving. The testing done by the adoption department as part of our home study had confirmed our belief that Dave had above average intelligence. He was an inquisitive child, and he asked several times how the baby was going to get out of my stomach.

Unfortunately, David's timing always seemed poor. His questions came when it was impossible for me to sit down and explain. One day he approached me again just as he and Bobby finished their lunch.

"Mommy, if a baby is growing in your tummy and that's why you look so fat, how will it get out?"

Bobby, pushing his chair back to leave the table, gave Dave a disgusted look and replied, "Don't you know? The 'docor' takes it out, stupid!" Bobby was satisfied with his own explanation, but four-year-old David persisted with more questions. I sat beside him and in simple detail explained what would transpire. Satisfied, he ran off to play.

I told Don that evening, "The boys gave me a real lesson in child raising today. David had to know how the new baby will get out, but not Bobby. His faith is in the 'docor,' with absolutely no interest in anatomy."

The date for the finalization of Bobby's adoption was pushed ahead, and our day in court arrived. David went to his grandparents for the morning while Don and I, with Bobby all dressed up to look like the little darling that he was, went to court.

I am petite and when I was not pregnant weighed in at just under one hundred pounds. When pregnant, however, I resembled an inflated dirigible. We strode into the courtroom and discovered that a dozen other couples were there for the same purpose. I felt extremely conspicuous, looking as if the next addition to our family might arrive before Bobby became legally ours. We were the first couple to be called forward, and I'm sure that the judge juggled papers to get us out of there quickly.

Bobby was finally ours! It was official. No one could take him away! When we arrived home, Mom had baked a cake for a real celebration. The boys ate ice cream, and Bobby blew out candles on the cake just as if it was a birthday party. It was a joyous occasion!

Two weeks later Donny was born. Despite my weight gain of forty pounds, he weighed in at only four pounds. "Mrs. Nyberg," Dr. Decker said when Donny arrived, "he's pretty enough to be a girl . . . but he isn't."

We weren't disappointed. Another son was wonderful! There was an exact twenty-five-month span between our boys. God had answered our prayers with a perfect family. Our prayer now was that the years to follow would be smooth. But this time God did not answer in the affirmative.

4
Sopping Saga

In the weeks following the court appearance Bobby's resistance to discipline became more obvious. Whenever I left the children with a babysitter, for example, I always explained, "Bobby wishes that the word 'no' were not a part of our language. He has difficulty distinguishing between right and wrong. You have to show Bobby that you're the boss. Don't let him get away with anything, or you'll lose out. Be strong and loving with the 'no,' but firm and consistent."

Often, his little fists clenched, Bobby would run screaming to his room and tear it apart. After each tantrum subsided, I would tell him, "Straighten up your room now if you want to come out and join the rest of the family."

One rainy day Bobby insisted on playing outside. I told him that it was too cold and that he must play indoors. Suddenly he began screaming, charged at me, and catapulted himself into my arms at full speed. He held his breath, his eyes rolled up, and he lost consciousness. I was terrified. Worried, I telephoned our doctor and asked him what to do about Bobby's newest manifestation.

"Bobby is an intelligent little boy," he told me. "I doubt that he is doing that on purpose *yet*, but he will learn to use it at will if he does it often enough. Stop the breath-holding any way you can before it becomes a habit."

Several days later Bobby tried again. He ran to me, scream-ing at a high pitch. I sat down and pulled him over my knees with his stomach on my legs. I rubbed his back vigorously while trying to soothe him. He could not hold his breath. In time this phase of his behavior passed. But he still had temper tantrums.

Whenever Don or I would deny the boys permission to do something, Donny and Dave would pout and stomp off angrily. But Bobby never gave up! He'd wheedle and wheedle. "Why can't we? Why can't we?" he'd shout. "You never let us do what we want to do!" On and on it would go. "No" meant "maybe" to Bobby, and he believed it worthwhile to try to change our minds. We never did, but he still continued to try to manipulate us.

After witnessing one of his rages, Mom suggested, "Can't you watch and see what it is that upsets him enough to turn him into such a little monster? Then try to avoid those situations."

"Mom," I replied, "I already know what sets him off. He loses his temper every time he is told 'no' to something he wants to have or do. He simply can't accept the fact that he can't always do as he pleases."

Bobby's need for immediate personal self-gratification was one of the first signs of the psychopathic personality he was later diagnosed as having. This was only the beginning of many personality problems and concerns that we would have to face.

Don has always been a tease. On many occasions when he and the boys would be stretched out on the floor to play together, Don would reach out and grab me by the ankle as I'd walk by.

"Knock it off!" I'd holler, bending down to try to release his iron grip. "Come on, I'm trying to get the house in order," I'd laughingly beg. "Let me go."

Whenever that happened, Bobby would fly to his dad with fists pummeling and scream, "Don't you hurt Mommy. Let her go!" Don would release me, grab Bobby, and lovingly ex-plain that he was just teasing me in the same way he teased the boys from time to time. Bobby, however, would not listen. He would continue to hit Don vehemently, shouting, "You were hurting Mommy!"

The other boys tried also to placate Bobby by saying, "Daddy is only playing with Mommy." But nothing would change Bobby's mind.

Once again I spoke to our ever-available family doctor about this latest problem. His advice was to cease the playfulness. "He may have witnessed something he remembers subconsciously that makes it impossible for him to understand physical teasing between you two. You have no idea what may have happened during his first year of life. It's too bad, but I'm afraid Don will have to be grown-up and formal with you in front of the kids."

It was a devastating decision for us to make. Don and I had been raised on teasing. It was a part of our lifestyle. We enjoyed it, and so did Donny and Dave. *Is it fair to the rest of the family,* we wondered, *to have to change our actions?* We ultimately decided that if teasing were so upsetting to Bobby, we had better heed Dr. Decker's recommendation. We became models of decorum whenever Bobby was around.

Although all three boys had been easy to toilet train, Bobby had a chronic problem with bedwetting. He was able to stay dry all day but woke up every morning soaking wet. He would detour via the bathroom to deposit his diapers and rubber pants in the tub before joining the family in our bed. It was a ritual to have the boys hop into bed with us before we all got up and started our day.

His bedwetting continued long after he had given up his bedtime bottle, which may have been the start of the problem. Again I took our problem to Dr. Decker, who advised me, "Ignore the situation. If he is still a bedwetter when he's ready to start kindergarten, we'll tackle the matter then."

When Bobby was five and still wetting the bed, Dr. Decker mapped out our plan of action. "We'll start the main attack when summer arrives, but meanwhile time Bobby during the day. I want to know how often he has to go the bathroom."

I was shocked when I discovered Bobby came running into the house every forty-five minutes like clockwork. He'd leave his trike down the block and run pell-mell to the bathroom. He *never* had a daytime accident, but his holding capacity was obviously minute. When I reported this fact to the doctor, he gave me my next instruction.

"When he comes running in, stop him or stall him. Try to read a story to him, anything to force him to hold on."

Because Bobby was in perpetual motion, it was next to impossible to read to him. I could stall him with a cookie. We also did not allow him any liquids after four o'clock.

Eventually the time span between his toilet treks was stretched out to an hour and then to an hour and a half. When Bobby reached two hours, we entered phase three and had a long talk with him.

"Dr. Decker, Mom, and Dad are thrilled with the progress you've made, Bobby. Now we are going to try something else."

"What?" Bobby asked, wide-eyed.

"How would you like to throw away the diapers and rubber pants and go to bed in pajamas just like your brothers?"

"Boy, I'd like that," he replied, "But will it work?"

He wasn't any happier with his morning ammonia aroma than we were, and he was also afraid other kids might learn about his problem. So that first night we tucked him into bed with no diapers under his pajamas and listened to his bedtime prayers. We thanked God for the progress he was making and also asked God to help him stay dry. I then set the alarm for two hours later.

When it rang, I entered his bedroon, woke him, and walked him to the bathroon. We were all pleased to find him dry. I reset the alarm for another two hours, and the time flew by. This time he was sound asleep in a puddle. I woke him anyway, as instructed, and we again trudged to the bathroom to be certain that his bladder was entirely empty. He was disappointed, but we encouraged him by emphasizing that this problem would take time to solve. I changed his pajamas and bedding and tucked him back into bed.

This routine continued night after night. Often he was dry; many times he was saturated. As he became dry more often

than sopping wet, we increased the time between alarm set-
tings. Eventually we woke him up when we went to bed and
again about two or three in the morning.

Although we were succeeding in breaking the bedwetting
habit, it was taking its toll on me. "I've about had it, Don," I exclaimed one night as I dropped back into bed after the nightly
alarm. "I don't know if it's worth all that this is taking out of me.
I'm sure Bobby will eventually dry up by himself. Grown men
don't wet their beds. He'll stop someday. I'm tired."

"Hey, I know this has been hard on you, but he's making
headway. We can't quit now. I'll take over the night runs if
they're too much for you. Or you can take naps in the daytime
to catch up on your sleep. But I won't let us stop now for
anything."

Problems such as this drew Don and me closer. Donny and
Dave, too, learned compassion. They never confided Bobby's
secret to any of the neighborhood kids, even when they were
mad at him.

It had been a rough procedure, but it was finally successful.
No one was happier than Bobby. He was now a more welcome
member in the community bed each morning. He had overcome his problem. His sleeping habits, however, had been
altered. Instead of sleeping soundly, he woke up at every noise
in the night. At the time we thought that these and similar problems were immense, and they were, but they were nothing
compared to what lay ahead.

5
Buffalo Bobby

When the big day arrived for Bobby to start school, he was looking forward to riding the school bus with the other kids in the neighborhood. The quiet, withdrawn, frightened little boy had long ago disappeared. He was still small, with blond curls and mischievous eyes, but he was bold and forward with his peers.

He skimmed through kindergarten without causing any problems for his teacher. "He is one of the sharp kids," she reported. "I feel he will do as well in school as David."

Bobby went off to first grade as pleased as he had been to start kindergarten. One afternoon he proudly brought home a piece of his work and exclaimed, "Look, Mommy, at what I wrote!"

"Where did you get this?" I asked, looking at the paper.

"I copied it off the blackboard," he replied.

I praised his work, and the next day I stopped at the school to talk to his teacher about it. The words had been perfectly copied, only each letter was reversed. The words could not be read unless they were held up to a mirror.

"Oh, that isn't unusual for first graders," Mrs. Brown replied in response to my question about Bobby's paper. "His writing won't stay that way. It often happens and is nothing to worry about." She was very reassuring. Although mirror writing is the first sign of dyslexia, we were unaware that such a problem even existed. The school sloughed it off as insignificant.

Midway into the fall session I received a note from Mrs. Brown asking me to come in for a conference. "Please sit down," she said as she opened the classroom door. "Bobby has a very serious problem, and I have called you in to recommend that you take him for psychiatric counseling."

I was stunned. I knew that Bobby could be a behavioral problem when he was not handled firmly. But . . . a psychiatric problem? I didn't comprehend that!

"He is upsetting the whole class," she continued, without even giving me a chance to gasp or reply. "He will not follow directions. He is disruptive, and yesterday was the final episode. When I release the children to the playground, I try to keep Bobby behind because he rushes out so fast he knocks other children down. But yesterday he rushed out of the classroom anyway. We had been watching a family of birds build a nest in that bush outside the window. The eggs were laid, and the mother bird was sitting on the nest. Bobby tore out there, grabbed the bush, knocked the nest down, and stomped on the eggs. The kids were so angry I thought they would murder him. I simply don't know what to do with Bobby. I don't understand his actions and cannot tolerate them in my class."

I felt numb. My thoughts whirled. I was speechless. *Bobby is an extremely energetic child, but . . . I just don't understand. I know Bobby can be a behavioral problem, but a psychiatric problem? What do I say? Oh, how I wish Don were here, too!*" We've been able to control Bobby at home with firmness and love," I stammered. "His kindergarten teacher had no problem with him. This is a shock!"

"Yes, I know. I talked to Miss Marshall, and she told me the same thing. He seems to have changed since then. He is completely unmanageable."

"Are you expelling him from first grade?" I asked in amazement.

"No, I can't do that, but I do sincerely feel that he is a *very* disturbed child and needs professional help."

"All I can say is that I'll discuss the situation with his father tonight. We'll have to reach some decision about what we feel is the best route to go. Tomorrow I'll talk to our family doctor about Bobby. I'll get back to you as soon as possible."

"Thank you. Something has to be done if he is to say in school."

I left the building feeling as though I had been run over by a steam roller. That evening Don and I talked and prayed long into the night and came up with no answers. We did decide, however, that if Dr. Decker felt it was the thing to do, we'd go the psychiatric route. Perhaps he could recommend a psychiatrist to whom we could take Bobby. We gave the problem to the Lord for the night and turned off the light to try to get some sleep.

The next morning Dr. Decker encouraged us to follow through with the psychiatrist, recommending one whose reputation with children was widely known in our city. We made an appointment for the following week.

The afternoon of the visit arrived. Bobby and I waited in the comfortable waiting room of the psychiatrist's deeply carpeted office suite. Soon we were ushered into his private office where he talked with both Bobby and me for a short time. Then he asked me to leave and I returned to the waiting room.

After about forty-five minutes he invited me back into the private office. Bobby left with the nurse to be entertained while I chatted with the doctor. "Bobby has an extreme complex," the doctor stated bluntly. "He feels inferior even to his younger brother. Could you please describe your other two sons for me?"

"David is an exceptionally bright child," I explained, "but Donny is just a normal kid like Bobby. Bobby has been somewhat of discipline problem at home, but not like his teacher has encountered at school."

"I want to run a battery of tests on Bobby," the doctor continued. "I want to discover what his I.Q. is and if they are pushing him too hard at school. He is seeking attention because of his inferiority feelings and uses bad behavior as a means of getting that attention.

An appointment for testing was made for the following week. When we arrived, the doctor introduced us to a tall, young man. "I'd like you to meet Mike Cleaver," he said. "He's a student who will do Bobby's testing." I was tempted to object, knowing Bobby's manipulative abilities, but decided it best not to interfere.

The test results were a further shock to me. "Bobby has an I.Q. of eighty," the doctor stated. "You and the school are pushing him and expecting him to keep up with his peers. It is impossible! If they will take the pressure off and let him enjoy school, he will straighten out and everything will be all right."

Sitting in that posh office, listening to his "correct analysis" of our son's problems, I wanted to scream and tell him he was wrong! One does not, however, tell an eminent psychiatrist that he is mistaken. I *knew* that Bobby was not borderline retarded. It angered me that a doctor would spend less than an hour with a child, have a young student run some tests, and then come up with a report that was so derogatory. Bobby had "buffaloed" the psychologist who had first tested him. She, however, had been more experienced and had recognized the fact. This time I was the only one aware of his "buffaloing."

When I discussed the results with Mrs. Brown, she, too, agreed with my opinion. "Bobby has an emotional problem," she said, "but he is not mentally below normal." The doctor had not recognized the dyslexia either, and it later proved to be a real trouble spot for Bobby. From that point on, he fell farther and farther behind in his learning.

6
Additional Psychiatry

Bobby's temper tantrums continued. Whenever Don or I would tell him "no," he yelled, "You just don't love me because I'm adopted."

I then quietly talked to him, trying to calm him when disciplining was necessary. "Bobby, are you being punished because you're adopted, or have you done something wrong?" I'd ask.

"Oh, I know. Stop asking me that silly question!" he'd reply.

"Okay, I'll make a pact with you. You stop your silly statement about why you're being punished, and I'll promise not to ask my silly question again. You know that you are disciplined no differently from your brothers."

"I know it," he'd answer, but he still told other people that we didn't love him and favored his brothers.

His school troubles also continued. His teachers still sought answers about what to do with him. He was learning nothing and daydreamed through second grade.

In an effort to better understand Bobby, I did some reading about adopted children and their particular problems. Eleanor Craig in her book *P.S. You're Not Listening* records a psychiatrist's discussion about adopted children. The psychiatrist states that many adopted youngsters have problems because their ability to learn is hampered by the energy invested in the longing for their natural parents. They unconsciously confuse *learning* with learning about *adoption*. With this in mind I kept thinking, *Is Bobby daydreaming about the unknown reality—his biological parents, that "charmer" father the social worker told us about?*

During summer vacation we took Bobby to Lillian Wakefield, an old family friend and elementary school teacher who had given I.Q. tests to children of all ages and types. "Lillian," I explained. "Bobby has been tested by two different 'experts' and their results have been different." I went on to describe the circumstances and asked her to test him.

Lillian tested Bobby, watching to see that he worked to his ability and didn't try to "buffalo" her. She reported, "Bobby's I.Q. is in the low average bracket. I'm certain he would test higher if he had applied himself these past two years in school. However, he is *far* from being retarded. I would suggest you take him to the Child Guidance Clinic for help."

We applied, but the clinic had a long waiting list, so it was almost a year before Bobby was accepted. During testing at the clinic, while Bobby was in the fourth grade, we first discovered that his learning problem was dyslexia. This medical problem affects a child's ability to read. According to current statistics, from three to five percent of the entire population suffers from dyslexia, which occurs most often among boys.

Children with dyslexia are not retarded, but their eye coordination will not permit them to read in a normal way. They do not visually see the letters from left to right. Many times the words are backwards or the letters are upside down. For example, "was," is "saw," "no" is "on," "left" is "felt," and "n" is "u." The tendency is believed to be hereditary, an interesting but impossible fact to verify in Bobby's case.

The clinic, in turn, referred us to a teacher in a neighboring city who specialized in working with children who have dyslexia. Bobby was enrolled, and each morning we left the house early to drive thirty miles so he could attend classes from eight to eleven o'clock. I would wait for him and return him to public school for his afternoon classes.

Under this special tutoring Bob learned to make himself

see the words from left to right, but another problem resulted. He began adding his arithmetic from left to right. This led to further difficulties, and his schoolmates left him far behind. He was passed from grade to grade simply because the school authorities didn't feel holding him back would help.

This special tutoring was time-consuming for me as well as a financial burden. Bob didn't seem to be making any progress. He lacked the personal drive necessary to achieve scholastically.

Even Bobby's psychiatrist at the Child Guidance Clinic seemed baffled. "Bob will only talk about surface things," he reported. "If I try to get into his deep feelings, he clams up."

Each time Bobby visited the clinic, I would talk with a social worker while the psychiatrist worked with him. After the first thorough researching of Bobby's problem, the social worker told me, "At first we looked for an easy solution, in that Bobby was a middle child. With Donny coming so soon after Bobby joined the family, we thought perhaps Bobby wasn't *really* wanted. But we now know that Bobby feels he is completely a part of your family, loved by you all. He only uses his adoption as a crutch. He is secure within the family structure."

Bobby began attending group therapy twice a week after school, and a psychologist worked with the children to see how they adjusted to playing together. I was interested to learn that of the eight children in the group, six of them were adopted. Through *P.S. You're Not Listening*, I had learned that professional psychiatrists see ten times as many adopted children as their proportionate number in the general population. *Do adopted children feel less secure, less able to cope with everyday living?* I wondered. *Do they spend too much time daydreaming about their biological parents?*

Soon I had to speak to Bobby's psychiatrist about another problem—thievery. "Oh, in a kid like him, that isn't stealing. I call it 'lifting.' It's something all kids do," he flippantly replied.

We first discovered Bobby's "lifting" when he accompanied me to a neighborhood drugstore. When we returned home, he ran off to play. Several days later I discovered him playing with a rubber dagger. "Where did you get that?" I questioned.

"Oh, I just got it," Bobby replied.

"Bobby, tell me where it came from. I did not buy it for you, and no one has given you a gift. Where did that dagger come from?"

After further discussion, he admitted, "I took it from the drugstore."

"You will have to return it to the store, tell the druggist you're sorry, and pay for it from your allowance because it is damaged." While Bobby continued playing outside, I telephoned the druggist to explain what had transpired and told him that I would bring Bobby in to return the dagger.

At the store Bobby turned on his charm. He smiled shyly, his head tipped at an innocent angle, his whole being a picture of remorse. "I'm sorry," he said. "I really am." His blue eyes were brimming with tears, and I stood and watched the druggist melt.

"That's all right, Bobby. I know you didn't mean to do wrong. You take the dagger home with you now. I'll give it to you." The electricity flashed on like a neon sign. Bobby turned and grinned at me. I could hear the wheels of his mind whirling —*it worked!*

His captivating charm had undone everything I had attempted to teach him through this incident. I became the ogre, insisting that he could not keep the knife and making him return it. Bobby had always been manipulative; this time it almost worked. Perhaps he filed this discovery away in his mind for future application because his thievery continued.

In spite of learning and discipline problems, Bobby was a normal young boy who wanted to do all the things other kids do. David was a cub scout, so Bobby decided he wanted to be one, too. Since all the·dens were filled to capacity and several boys were waiting for space, it was suggested that I become a den mother. I still have the scars and den mother pin to prove the honor. My den was filled with all the boys no one else wanted. It was a full-time job trying to keep them from wrestling the whole time we were together. Young boys aren't too interested in doing crafts, and mine weren't singers, either. They seemed to have no talent for anything but fighting.

My assistant appeared for only one session, and by the end of the year I was exhausted. I felt it was time for another mother to have the privilege of keeping a dozen boys busy. A new leader was drafted, and at the second meeting she kicked Bob out of the den. Even though her son had been one the "wild" ones I had struggled with for the entire year, she wouldn't even try to deal with Bobby. It made me furious! I was relieved that Bobby didn't seem to care; his short attention span had reached its capacity for cubbing.

During this time Bobby's counseling continued. On one of our clinic days I spoke to the social worker about a plan that Don and I had developed. "We have been talking about becoming foster parents," I explained. "We thought it might help Bob understand the adoption situation better if we demonstrated how babies are placed in foster homes, loved totally, and then established in permanent homes,"

"That sounds like a good idea," she replied. "I'm sure you'd be welcomed into the program. But be certain that you can emotionally handle giving up the child when final placement is made."

"It will be an adjustment, I know, but remember, we have been on the other side. We know the happiness adoptive parents have when a child is finally their very own." I continued, "The knowledge of that personal feeling will dull any hurt we may experience. We have already talked about it."

About two weeks later Children's Home Society welcomed us into their foster parent program and licensed our home for one infant at a time. We were the overflow home. If more babies arrived than normal, we would get one. Before long a call came.

"Mrs. Nyberg, we have a new baby girl, just born today. She will be ready to go home at the end of the week. Could you take her?"

"You bet we will," I stated. "A little girl in this house will be something special." She was beautiful. We named her Susy and loved her completely. A few months later she was placed in her permanent home. When she left, we all shed tears of sadness and joy. We knew what was taking place in the new parents' hearts.

Altogether, we cared for about a dozen babies, and each found a special place in our lives. It was an excellent experience for all three boys. They saw how each baby was loved individually, without being a part of our family by birth or legal adoption. They learned that love meant the pleasure of being allowed to care for the babies until their placement in permanent homes. The boys helped by fetching bottles and diapers, and entertaining each baby when it was fussy. It was a happy experience for us all.

But this, too, ended. Don caused turbulence at the dinner table one evening by asking, "How would you all feel about packing up and moving to the west coast?"

7

Growing Bob, Growing Problems

A few weeks later Don and I boarded a jet to check out the area of our proposed move. We spent several days looking over the countryside and investigating housing. Don also devoted time to his prospective employers. It was a pleasant respite from our daily chores, even though we were saturated with decision-making. We headed home bursting with ideas, questions, and choices to be considered.

"I wonder if God has put this opportunity in our laps for Bob as well as for you, Don?"

"What do you mean by that?"

"Well, I have a feeling that the staff members at Child Guidance Clinic would be relieved if I told them we were taking Bob out of the program. I'm wondering, too, if a change of location and new friends might not be good for him."

"Leave his reputation behind, you mean? Maybe that would help, but why the feeling about the clinic?"

"I honestly think they don't know where to go with him. You remember what his psychiatrist said about the deep feelings Bob won't share. I'm certain the staff members are against a wall, hate to admit defeat, and would be relieved to have us move away. Why is this child such a riddle to everyone? It's frightening to think that Bobby can even buffalo the psychiatrists. I'm frustrated!"

"Don't worry about Bob. He'll make out all right with his charm. And as to the move, we'll just have to wait and see what transpires."

"I hope Mom and Dad have survived having the kids full time."

"Your parents can handle Bob. Have no fear about that. We'll find they had a great time and will hate to see us back."

As our plane landed and taxied to a stop, we saw Mom, Dad, and the boys waving excitedly to us from the airport waiting area. It had been great fun to get away, but it was even better to be home again.

"Are we going to move?" the boys chorused as we embraced them all.

"We don't know yet. Dad will decide for sure next week. It's beautiful country, and we saw lots of houses we'd be happy to live in. I know you kids would love it there, too."

The following week, we reached a decision—the Nyberg family was westward bound. We sold our home quickly and moved out. The drive west was uneventful, and we arrived at our destination brimming with anticipation. *What new adventures*, we thought, *will this era of our lives unfold?* We located a suitable house that would be available for occupancy before school started. If our furniture arrived on schedule, we'd be settled and ready.

I then approached the school principal with the question of holding Bob back a year. I didn't want to introduce his history of disrupting classes, but I knew all his records would be available to the new teacher. I explained that his scholastic troubles were partially due to dyslexia, and the principal decided to have Bob repeat the fifth grade.

In the new school the fifth grade pupils were divided into two sections: easy learners and those with difficulties. This proved to be unfortunate for Bob. It didn't help him to be surrounded by others kids with behavioral and learning problems. He regressed.

According to Dr. Rudolph F. Wagner's book *Dyslexia and Your Child*, many parents hold their children back in school to help them with their reading problems, just as we had done. Instead of receiving special help, however, the children are again exposed to the same teaching they had the previous year. Because it is not easier, the student often becomes bored, listless, and resentful. This attitude doesn't lessen behavioral problems in the classroom.

After school started, Bob began to express interest in joining Boys Club of America. The club met one evening a week at the school. He was enrolled with our blessing and kicked out after two meetings for being disruptive. It was a repeat of his scouting experience.

When your child hurts, you as a parent hurt. As much as we were perplexed about Bob's problems, it was shattering to see him hurt by people who should have been helping him. In frustration I picked up the telephone and called my parents, who loved Bob unconditionally. "I'm so mad and hurting for Bob that I just have to call and talk to someone I can spout off at."

"What's happened?" Mom asked.

"Bob's been tossed out of Boy's Club, just like in Scouts. These organizations are supposed to help kids, not give up on them so quickly."

"True. But remember that they don't have professionals as leaders. They're just normal people who have bad days and short fuses at times. How did Bob take it?"

"Oh, you know Bob's bravado. He hides his hurt. He said, 'I didn't want to go anyway. It's just a bunch of dumb kids.'"

As we neared the end of our conversation and said goodby, Mom stated, "God will take care of the hurt. Pray for the leader, because he may be hurting more than any of us."

Another continuing problem area was Bob's pilfering. We learned to keep our billfolds hidden. After keeping close track and listing amounts, we realized we were constantly being relieved of cash in spite of our caution. At the grocery store I would find only one five dollar bill when I was certain there had been two. Even when caught in the act of stealing, Bob would deny what he had done.

Bob also "lifted" items to keep his female friends happy.

Two of my treasured family heirloom jewelry pieces disappeared during this period. They were of no great monetary value, but they were sentimental favorites of mine. Long after there was any possibility of recovery, Bob admitted having given them to a girlfriend.

About this time we found more desirable property and decided to move again. In the Midwest a move had meant only adjusting to a new home while the children remained in the same school. Now, in this more expansive area, our move meant a new neighborhood and a different school.

This time the change was an improvement for Bob. Our home was in the country, the school smaller, and his teacher concerned about his scholastic problems. He was enrolled in the seventh grade but was so far behind it seemed an impossible task to get him moving toward his grade level. Although he was no longer disruptive, his teachers still struggled to find things to hold his interest.

We met with the school administrators and decided to place Bob in the work-school program. He was given a job in a neighboring filling station where he had the opportunity to learn simple auto mechanics and the basics of running a business. Bob enjoyed the work, learned to change oil and grease cars. But the "lifting" problem his psychiatrist had ignored was his downfall.

He soon began helping himself to change from the cash register, and the school was forced to withdraw him from that portion of the program. Now they felt as boxed in with him as we did. His attention span was so limited that he could not cope with the tasks given other students. He was almost illiterate.

One evening after the boys were asleep Don and I tried once again to figure out what to do for Bob. "What's bothering me now, Don, is Bob's choice of friends. The kids he brings home appear to be borderline delinquents. He seems to attract that kind of friend."

"What about the kids at church?" Doesn't Bob know any of them at school?" Don asked.

"Yes, but he says they're a year ahead of him. They're nice

to him at church, but they ignore him at school."

"Kids that age are funny. I suppose they think he's dumb. If he had to stand up and read aloud in class, you know what they'd think. The teacher can't excuse him from everything the others do."

"If only he could excel at sports. That would give him an interest."

"I think he could, if he would apply himself," Don continued. "He seems to lack interest in anything except goofing off."

"Most of his pals obviously lack discipline at home and are real troublemakers at school. I try hard to be loving toward them when Bob brings them here. I'm sure most of them lack love at home."

"He's never kept friends very long; maybe this group will move on, too. It's impossible for us to choose his pals, but we can encourage him to associate with the kids we do approve of from church."

Even though it is difficult to love unconditionally, we loved Bob and prayed he would let God take over his young life. We hurt for the barbs he was taking, but we couldn't blame other kids and their parents for their feelings. We prayed that somewhere someone would be able to love him unconditionally and through that loving acceptance help him.

At conference time Bob's teacher remarked, "He is becoming really obnoxious. He used to be sweet and so willing to help whenever I gave him a chore. Now he is arrogant and loud-mouthed, and the kids call him a hot-aired braggart! I know many little children fight for attention by being naughty, but now Bob is getting it by being impossible. I love him and feel sorry for him, but I would like to shake him sometimes. He stretches the truth beyond its elasticity. I'm about at the end of my tolerance."

Our tolerance was also being tested, but we knew our young son needed love and direction. With the help of God we knew we'd all survive.

Jim, a member of our church, was the chaplain at the

Youth Diagnostic Center. Every child who got into police trouble was sent to the center for diagnostic testing before sentencing. The staff was accustomed to kids worse than Bob. Jim knew Bob from Sunday school and Youth Fellowship. He volunteered to take him in on a slow day and run a battery of tests on him.

Bob went off with him happily one Saturday. Later Jim reported, "Bob has his dyslexia under control and could work himself up to grade level *if* he would apply himself. He simply lacks motivation. I want to add one thing for you and Don to remember. If Bob doesn't make it in this world, don't crucify yourselves. If he'd been tossed back and forth between his biological parents, he could not have made it. Only being placed in a stable home has given him the opportunity to get as far as he has. Now remember what I have said when things get rough."

How those words comforted us as the years rolled along. Bob continued to accomplish nothing in school, and his companions were not a good influence. I was upset and worried about him, still struggling with my inability to completely leave his problems in God's hands.

In 1963 the days following the tragedy of the John F. Kennedy assassination were some of the lowest in my life. The news comentators kept harping on the fact that if Mrs. Oswald, Lee's mother, had only taken him for psychiatric help when he was young, the tragedy might have been avoided. *But,* I kept saying to myself, *Lee Harvey Oswald had been in no real trouble previously.* I wanted to pummel the television screen and scream. "It would have done her no good! Professionals feel that kids like this are not potential troublemakers. One has to wait until a person gets into big trouble before authorities become concerned."

I didn't consider our son to have the potential to become a killer, but I felt angry, bitter, and fearful of Bob's future. *To say Mrs. Oswald should have asked for help is ridiculous,* I kept thinking. *She wouldn't have been given any. Lee would have been patted on the head and told that stealing is only lifting.* I was bitter!

My own turbulence was analagous to the agitation of the times. The late sixties brought disruptions on college campuses; the God-is-dead philosophy emerged; drugs were appearing on school grounds. Discipline was ignored, and even little children were affected by their rebellious seniors.

When David was a junior in high school in 1964, the principal called me in. "Dave has had two years each of Latin and German, and trigonometry," he said. "There are no higher math or language courses available. He only lacks his senior English class to graduate. I would suggest he graduate with the seniors, take his English in summer school, and enter college in the fall."

Bob was in the eighth grade, a year behind because we had held him back. The two year spacing of our sons was off balance. Donny was now only a year behind Bob, and Dave was four years ahead of him. These facts increased Bob's inferiority complex. To hide his real feelings, he became more aggressive.

When Bob completed ninth grade, we knew the school system was ready to throw him out. We started searching for a private school. Directed to one that worked with boys with learning disorders, we drove the one hundred and fifty miles to investigate. Our first impression was good. The school might fit Bob's needs, we thought. Classes are small. Students work at their own level, progressing at their individual speed. The campus was not elaborate. It was situated outside the city in a rolling hillside area. The grass was green and well kept and the school building was old but clean. It was a Christian school.

The administrators were explicit in their questioning as to whether Bob had been in police trouble. They did *not* take boys with records, but Bob had none at that time. We saw students lounging around the grounds and buildings, laughing and talking together. Jeans and T-shirts were the costume of the day, and we knew that would appeal to Bob. He always resisted getting dressed up for anything; he reveled in being grubby.

On our second visit we took Bob along to let him tour the facilities. "Well, Bob, what do you think?" I asked as Don turned the car toward home.

"I like it," he answered. "I want to go if I can. The guys seemed nice. Even the teachers acted like they'd be nice to me."

Bob was enrolled in the tenth grade, and I was relieved to know he would be away from home for a school year. "What kind of a mother am I?" I asked Don. "I am so relieved to have Bob going away."

"Don't feel guilty now," Don said softly. "Bob has been a trial to us all, but you have taken the brunt of it. The change will be good for the whole family."

At age seventeen Bob's diminutiveness had disappeared. He was nearly six feet tall, filled out, and strong. The childhood tantrums had turned into scenes of glaring hatred flashing from Bob's blue eyes whenever he was denied his wish. His threats were becoming frightening to me. I didn't know how to cope with them. He would threaten, "I wish I could smash my fist into your face!"

"Bob," I'd answer, "if you want to hit me so badly, go ahead, but it will be the first and last time you ever do."

Then I'd turn away, praying that I had handled the situation correctly. Bob would stand fuming with his fists clenched until he cooled off. He never threatened me in front of Don, nor did he threaten him. Bob was not brave with someone his own size or larger.

His psychiatrist had warned me long before, "Now that Bob is getting bigger than you, leave all corporal punishment up to his dad. The only criticism I can give of your handling of Bob is that Don should have floored him, slugging him so hard he would understand what strict discipline is." I knew, though, that Don could not do that; he is not a vengeful person. He could never hit someone he loved that way. I still question the wisdom behind that suggestion. God teaches discipline with love, not abuse.

After every "toe to toe" session with Bob, I was physically and emotionally drained. As soon as I felt the household was calm enough, I'd announce, "I'm going to take a long, soaking bath. Please cover the phone and take any messages." Then I'd crawl into the hot tub, lie on the bottom submersed in water, and let the tears flow.

Saltwater tears mixed with steam became a balm for my troubled mind. I prayed fervently, "God, forgive my feelings toward this son. Forgive me for pulling the problem back from you, out of your loving and caring arms. Enfold Bob and me together so that my frustrations will not turn to hatred for this son. Father, he is one of your children, and you love him despite his disobedience. Help me to do likewise. Forgive me for my inability to cope. Thank you for all the strength you give me each day."

Renewed by my prayer time, the relaxing comfort of the hot water, and the release of emotions through my sobbing flow of tears, I could return to the world outside my locked bathroom door. There I could pick up the pieces of my shattered emotions and walk out to face the rest of the day.

8
Fractured Skull

We packed up Bob's belongings with love, praying that we were not doing the wrong thing. I needed a rest from Bob's abusiveness and threats. Surely this year at school *had* to be God's directive.

The car was piled full of Bob's treasures and clothes as we turned out of the driveway and started on our way to Bob's new destination.

"How does it feel to be going away to school?" I asked.

"Great! I'll miss you guys, but I'm glad I decided to go."

Bob was excited at the prospect of going away, off on a new adventure. He almost seemed relieved to be getting away from the family; the static had been building up for him, too.

After a pleasant trip we arrived at the school and helped Bob unpack. The other boys in the dorm seemed polite and friendly, and we felt comfortable with our decision. After settling Bob into his room and meeting the staff, we departed for home.

David had already left for his sophomore year of college, returning to the state of his birth where grandparents, uncles, and aunts resided. He had always been very independent, and everyone felt secure about his starting college at age seventeen. He had his life path planned; he would travel it with ease and happiness.

We were a diminshed family of only three people. This solo experience proved helpful for Donny, who was shy. He did well in school, but he had to work to attain the honors Dave gained so easily. Donny was also burdened with Bob's undesirable reputation. On many occasions Bob had threatened to "annihilate" Donny. Now life continued in our peaceful triumvirate.

Bob's letters were few but cheerful. The reports from the administrative office were glowing. "Bob is attaining slow but steady success in his learning process. We are delighted to report that he has gone forward at chapel and given his life to the Lord."

We were delighted to hear the good news, but we held reservations. Bob had always attended Sunday school, Youth Fellowship, and all church functions. His knowledge of the Lord had been part of his training at home. We knew that he would go forward at a service if the act would earn the praise of his teachers. We prayed that his commitment was sincere.

In one of his letters, Bob wrote:

Dear Mom and Dad, I went up at chapl when the minster ask us to I lik it her but sum of the guys arnt good. Love Bob

His spelling hadn't improved, and we were puzzled by his statement about the other boys. We felt concern but had no concrete reasons for the feelings.

The sound of the telephone interrupted our dinner conversation later that week. "Hello," Don answered. "No! Is it serious?"

I ran to an extension phone in time to hear the headmaster's wife continue, "Bob was hurt on the playground this afternoon and has been taken to the hospital."

"How badly is he hurt?" I questioned.

"He really is fine; don't worry. They only hospitalized him as a precaution."

"Should we drive right down?" Don asked.

"No, he's sedated and sleepy. He's all right. But I thought

I'd better let you know what happened."

"What did happen?" we both chorused.

"The boys were playing on the school grounds, and somebody threw a piece of wood. It was a freak accident. It just happened to hit Bob. His head was bleeding profusely as scalp wounds will do, so we took him to the doctor to be sewn up. He fainted while he was there, and the doctor felt that he should be hospitalized to be safe. He'll no doubt be released in the morning."

"Tell him you talked to us, we love him, and we'll be down first thing in the morning."

"I'll do that," she replied, "but please don't worry. I questioned even calling; it is such a minor injury. We'll see you tomorrow then."

We went to bed early, planning to leave at dawn and arrive early enough to intercept the doctor before he made his rounds. At 7:45 we walked into the hospital. The woman at the reception desk smiled in relief when we gave her our name. "I've been trying to reach you since six," she stated. "The doctor wants to see you immediately."

Fear clutched our hearts as we hurried to meet the doctor. "Your son has a fractured skull," he informed us in a gentle tone. "I don't foresee any danger, but he must undergo immediate surgery to remove a splinter of his skull that is pressing into the brain. I don't anticipate any lasting damage, but it must be removed. We need your permission to perform the surgery."

"What is the possibility of brain damage?" My mouth was dry as I verbalized my fear.

"The fracture is in the area affecting his speech. There is a slight possibility of speech damage. However, I feel that would be very unlikely. We can't really be sure of anything until we get him into surgery."

"We were told yesterday that he was fine, only hospitalized as a precaution." Don seemed to be trying to convince the doctor that nothing was really wrong.

"Apparently the school doctor thought Bob only had a laceration, which is a normal assumption. He gave him a shot of

Novocain to prepare him for suturing, and Bob passed out. He was given oxygen and rushed here by ambulance. He regained consciousness soon after he arrived and seemed fine. During the night checks a nurse discovered that his eyes weren't focusing. Further X-rays revealed a depressed fracture on the left side of the skull. The surgery will take a long time, so don't worry about the time span. Bob will be fine."

"May we see him first?"

"Yes, he's waiting for you. I have already talked to him and explained what we are going to do. He seems ready and has no fear."

We entered Bob's room. He smiled drowsily at us and said, "Did you hear that I broke my head? The doctor said he's going to fix it, though."

"That's what he told us, too," we replied. "We'll be right here waiting for you to come back to your room. And remember, God will be there with you."

"I know. I sure am sleepy," he replied.

Soon the nurses wheeled him off to surgery, and we settled down in the waiting room. I could feel the presence of the hundreds who had preceded us, detained in similar conditions. We waited for what seemed an eternity, but we had given Bob to the Lord many years before, and we rested in the knowledge that he was guiding the surgeon's scalpel.

Two and a half hours later the doctor entered the room. "Bob is going to be fine. The splinter missed the speech area by a fraction. He will be as active as ever in a few days. He has a small hole in his skull that will remain. We can put a steel plate in it, but that will mean further surgery at a later date. Frankly, the hole is over the large muscle in his head, and the chance of that particular spot ever being penetrated is extemely slim. You can think about it, and if you'd feel better if it were done, let me know. My advice would be to forget it."

"Thank you so much, doctor. We appreciate your giving up your Saturday to care for our son."

"That's my job," he replied, smiling. "Could you stay here, Mrs. Nyberg? It would be comforting for him to know that family is near. He'll be hospitalized about a week."

"Can I find a place nearby to stay?" I asked.

"Talk to the receptionist. Several people in the area rent rooms. I'll see you tomorrow."

"I'll be here." I wondered how I'd arrange it, and then realized I was trying to run things again. God was in charge, and he would do it.

We walked down the corridor to Bob's room, where nurses were bustling around keeping track of his vital signs. His bed was surrounded by strange equipment. We were aware that we were in the way, but we wanted to talk with him for a minute to reassure ourselves that he was okay.

Bob lay in bed, his head swathed in bandages. He opened his eyes, and a big tear rolled down his cheek. His voice was slurred from the anesthetic, but he grabbed my hand with an iron grip and said, "Oh, Mom, they cut off all my hair!"

Don winked at me, and we both grinned. Bob was all right—no brain damage here. His first concern was his baldness. Just another accident to chalk up to an already acquired multitude. He was our accident-prone son. He'd been stitched and X-rayed and bandaged so often, we hardly thought this mishap surprising.

"We're going home now," I explained, "but I'll be back first thing in the morning, Bob. I'll stay near the hospital until you can go home." We then arranged for a room in a comfortable home directly across the street from the hospital.

During the drive home I made lists of what I would have to do in order to return. Don and Donny would be bachelors for a week. When we arrived, I dashed into the house, washed clothes, packed lunches for Donny, and put them in the freezer along with dinner menus. After arranging for neighbors to know that I would be gone, I fell into bed exhausted.

At the first sign of light I headed south to see Bob. As I listened to a Sunday sermon on the car radio, I praised God for his goodness to us all. After settling into my room, I hurried across to the hospital. Bob was sitting up in bed, resembling a turbaned Indian. He was the center of attention and enjoying every minute of it. We talked about how glad we were that God had been with him.

The doctors released Bob five days later, and we set out for home. A blue surgical cap hid his shaven head and stitches. He was proud of that cap but also fearful of being teased about his bare skull. As we stopped at his school to gather some clothing, I felt a churning in my heart and mind about the school. *What had really happened? Should Bob return?* From my conversation with the headmaster, it seemed he was questioning the advisability of Bob's returning, although he didn't verbalize it.

"The doctor didn't say when Bob can return to school," I told the headmaster. "Will you pray with us for God's guidance in this decision? He certainly has been with Bob." We were aware it would be extremely difficult for Bob to reenter public school in midterm. He would be losing several weeks of school wherever he continued.

I registered my doubts to Don that evening. "There is nothing concrete, just my hunch about the accident. The headmaster's attitude today added to my growing misgivings about the school. He gave such glowing reports about Bob's progress, but we can't see it. Bob's remarks about some of the boys disturb me, especially after the school's emphasis on not taking in boys with police records. And now this accident. It doesn't make sense."

"Let's go to bed now. You're too tired to be thinking about all this tonight. Tomorrow it will all seem less dubious."

But thoughts continued to rotate through my brain during the night. I woke up exhausted. "Don," I said, as we sat at the breakfast table alone, "what about Bob's going back to the school? I'm still in a quandary about the situation there."

"I think it should be left up to Bob to decide," Don replied. "He's the one who would have to adjust to getting back into public school at midterm. Let's leave it up to him. He's old enough to make the decision."

"Yes, you're right . . . but let's ask God to help him decide."

Bob chose to return. We again retraced our journey south to the school. The remainder of the term passed quietly. When I pressed Bob for details of the accident, he repeated the same story that the school authorities had given me. I still questioned its validity.

June arrived, and with it came the end of the school year. We drove to retrieve Bob and his belongings. He waved good-bye to his friends and teachers, who felt he had made academic progress. We weren't so sure. His letters had not shown any improvement in grammar, spelling, or usage.

When Bob settled into the routine of summer, I gently questioned him. "Bob, tell me about the accident. You are so lucky not to have been hurt seriously. What happened to the boy who threw the board?"

"I don't know what happened to him," Bob replied. "He left the school." Further questioning gave Don and me no more answers.

In later years Bob reported that the headmaster had fabricated the story. In actuality the boy had deliberately hit Bob because Bob had been teasing him. He was a boy with a history of assault with weapons, and the police came and took him away. None of the other boys knew for certain what happened to him, but it was rumored that he was incarcerated because he was on probation for assault.

Because Bob has always been a weaver of tales, the true story may never be known. We thought at the time it had to have been a deliberate assault to have caused so much damage. I had been shown the board. It was a weather-beaten two-by-four with some of Bob's blond hair wedged in the splintered wood. I had stronger misgivings.

When we discussed the accident with Bob, we stressed God's loving compassion and how dependent we must all be on his help every day of our lives. God had been with us through that experience, and Bob was fortunate not to have been more seriously hurt.

As summer drew to a close, a decision about school had to be made. "Bob, we have to start thinking about school. You'll be in the eleventh grade, but your reading abilities and other skills are far behind. The only alternative to another year in the private school is the 'special' class in public school." (The class was for retarded children, but Bob *was* working at their level.)

"I don't think I want to go back to that school."

"The decision is up to you. If you go into the special class, you will have to take a lot of teasing from kids. They may call you retarded."

"I'm not, though, so I don't care," he replied.

Bob entered the special class in September, and it turned out to be his happiest year in school. He was at the top of the class, able to help the other students with their work. For once he was the best.

But his companions after school were not the best and led him into deeper trouble.

9
Mom, the Informant

During his junior year in high school Bob had his first encounter with the law. Many times during his life he has chosen the wrong kind of friend. Those he was associating with at that time were the most detrimental.

"Can't you find some different friends, Bob?" I asked.

"What's wrong with them? They like me."

"Bob, the kids would all like you if you gave them a chance. You're the sweetest boy in our family when you want to be. You have a built-in thoughtfulness that is natural for you. God gave you the ability to care for others, and when you are obedient to him you're a super kid. You can have the *right* kind of friends if you'll let them see this side of your personality." Bob only grunted in reply.

One day Bob failed to come home from school. By one o'clock in the morning, he still hadn't returned. He'd threatened to run away thousands of times in his growing years and our thoughts went back to Dr. Decker and his sound advice. At one time I told him of Bob's threats and added, "I actually feel like packing his bags and sending him off."

"Don't ever let him drive you to that point," he advised. "As bad as he gets, never let him run away. Do you know what happens to young boys who leave their homes?"

"No, what?"

"They wander the streets looking hungry and frightened. Sex perverts can spot them anyplace, pick the boys up, take them home and feed them, and are nice to them for a few days. Then they lead the boys into sex acts, and before the youngsters know what has happened to them, they are male prostitutes. Soon they are too ashamed to try to go home. Don't ever make it easy for Bob to run away."

The 1970s brought the very thing the doctor had warned us about. We didn't want Bob mixed up with a possible police record, but paralyzing thoughts went through our minds. *He had threatened so many times to run. Has he? Is he hurt somewhere and unable to get help?* Don and I mulled over the situation while pacing the floor and consuming gallons of coffee. We ultimately decided to call the police.

The following morning an officer telephoned to report they had found no sign of Bob. "Do you think he might be at school today?" the officer suggested.

"He just might at that. I'll drive over and check if you want me to."

"Please do and let me know. We'd rather not appear at school looking for him. It would be better if you went."

"Okay, I'll go right away and call when I return."

I drove to the school and went directly to the principal's office. I explained why I was there and that I didn't want Bob to know I was checking. The principal called to Bob's teacher on the intercom and asked him to report to the office.

When the teacher arrived, the principal asked if Bob was in class.

"Yes, Bob's there, and I wondered about him. He is so grubby. When I asked him about his appearance, he told me that he had camped out overnight." His teacher returned to the classroom with instructions to say nothing to Bob about the situation. I went home and reported to the police officer.

"If he comes home on the bus as usual," the officer said, "give me a ring and we'll close the book on the case unless you want us to investigate further. He probably did sleep out with some kids and will return home as usual."

After discussing the situation with Don, we decided I would pick Donny up early. We didn't want Bob questioning him about what we had done the previous night. Donny and I watched the bus turn down our street and let the kids out. Bob was among them. He swaggered across vacant lots, came in the side door, stomped through the kitchen, and without a word headed for his bedroom.

"Hey, wait a minute," I said. "Do you think that you can just reappear with no explanation of where you've been and expect no questions to be asked?"

"You can ask, but I'm not telling anything. It's none of your business because I don't live here anymore. I just came for clean clothes. I have a better place to live." He did not look at me.

"Do you expect to live elsewhere and only stop by when you need clean laundry?"

"Yup. I've got a good home to stay in, a place where they like me, and I don't need you guys!"

"Bob, you are a minor. We are responsible for you. You can't just walk out and drop in when your clothes are dirty. We reported you as a runaway last night when you didn't come home. The police still have a pickup notice on you."

Bob swung around and glared at me with the same hatred that appeared whenever he was thwarted. "I might have known you'd do a stupid thing like that. You never did love me. Well, I hate you all! I never want to see you again! I'm leaving for good; don't try to stop me or find me. I'm with a friend who likes me, and we get along good. So forget it. You just call the police and tell them to drop dead!"

He stalked through the house to his room and changed his clothes. He left the dirty ones on the floor and returned through the kitchen. Over his shoulder he shouted his last order—interspersed with some of his favorite four-letter words. "Wash the dirty clothes! I'll be back when I need them." He slammed the door and left.

I knew what I had to do. It isn't easy for a mother to turn her own son in to the police, but I knew Bob had to learn that he could not flout authority. I phoned the officer who had talked to me earlier. "Bob came home on the school bus, came in for clean clothes, and has taken off again. If you want him, he is walking across the golf course toward the highway."

"Thanks," he replied. "We'll pick him up and keep in touch."

Donny and I watched the police car pull up where Bob was walking and stop. The officer got out, talked to Bob, and then put him in the back seat of the squad car and drove off. My heart was in my toes. *Have I done the right thing? Where is it all going to end?"*

Later I received a telephone call. "Mrs. Nyberg, we have your son in custody. He is extremely angry that you reported him and is cussing you out but good. We are going to keep him overnight. If we release him to you, he will simply take off again. A night in jail will cool him off."

The overnight stay in jail was unnerving for Bob. He admitted later that he and some other boys had broken into a cabin and stolen guns and beer. The rest of his buddies were picked up. Bob remained angry with me for months, repeatedly stating, "It's all your fault for reporting me to the cops. The other guys are going to get you for it." He would not acknowledge that *he* had done wrong. As far as Bob was concerned, *we* were guilty for having reported him missing.

When we left him alone for a few hours several times during the summer, Bob hot-wired one of our cars and went joy riding with this same group of kids. He could never understand why that upset us or why he was punished as a result. If we took privileges away from him as punishment, he just bided his time until they were removed and started all over again.

The day of Bob's court appearance arrived. He was the only boy with both parents present. Our youth minister also attended. The judge talked to the boys and questioned each of them thoroughly about their experiences on the evening they had broken into the cabin. He asked Bob, among other things, "Did you have sexual relations with the girls who were with you?"

"Sure!" Bob answered, with a smugness that was sickening. Our young son, who we thought had learned some morals in our home, was proud and haughty about his sexual experiences. Don and I exchanged glances. *Where did we fail?*

Later the judge asked each mother the question, "Has your son ever been a discipline problem to you at home?"

I answered with a simple, "Yes."

As the other mothers were asked, they all answered, "No, never!"

This was the first time I had seen Bob fail to captivate anyone for his own advantage. His charm vanished in his venomous replies to the judge's questions. He projected his glaring hatred for me—the informer—onto the judge, spewing his bitterness with each answer.

Although the other boys were scolded, it was no surprise to me that Bob was the only one who was sentenced to the Youth Authority. His defiance had clearly influenced the judge's decision. The sentence was suspended, however, on three conditions. He must remain in school until he graduated. He must stay out of trouble. He must not associate with any of the other youngsters involved in the break-in.

On the way home Bob pounded the back of my seat with his fist. "Why did you say 'yes?' The other kids' mothers didn't squeal on them. That proves you don't love me."

I could reply with questions. "Did you do anything wrong to get you into this predicament? Have you ever been a discipline problem? Have you threatened to hit me when I tell you that you can't do something? Would you really expect me to lie for you? I would not lie for you, your brothers, or your dad."

Bob ignored my questions and continued to pound the seat. Finally, Don spoke up. "Stop that, Bob. Sit down like a gentleman. I have heard enough for one day. We all love you and will stick with you through all this, but in return I expect some respect from you for your mother and the rest of the family."

As the school year neared its end and summer approached, Don and I tried to figure out what Bob should do. He had attempted camp almost every summer for a week or two, but he was now too old for camping programs. Feeling that a summer job would be in his best interest, we lined one up through a friend.

Bob's job was washing cars at an auto dealership. He enjoyed the work and the opportunity to drive so many different kinds of cars to the wash area. One day, however, he backed one car into another, dented both autos, and simply walked away without reporting the incident. This action cost him his job. Our friend tried to explain to Bob that if he had been honest and reported what had happened, he wouldn't have been fired. But the novelty of the job was wearing thin, and Bob didn't mind being out of work.

A neighbor who was leaving town for a few days asked Bob to feed their dog and pick up the mail. She agreed to pay him for his services. When she returned, she telephoned me. "Dorothea, I hate to tell you this, but Bob broke into our house when we were gone, stole some silver dollars out of our coin collection, and spent them at the clubhouse. Ben, the cashier, recognized them and saved them for us so there was no loss to us. I felt that I had to tell you."

"Will you please call his probation officer and tell him? Mr. Jackson is his name, and he has to be told."

"I couldn't do that," she replied.

"We'll, if you won't, I will have to. Believe me, it isn't easy, but that is a condition of his parole. We are responsible to report anything he does wrong, or we're as guilty as he is. If you won't tell, I will have to."

"I just couldn't," she insisted.

Once again I had to be the ogre. I called and reported the theft. Mr. Jackson was at our home within the hour. Bob admitted the incident, and he was taken into custody.

Later Mr. Jackson called to say that he had put Bob to work painting some walls at Juvenile Hall and thought he should stay there for a few days. He also added, "I'm going to try to make him consider joining the army. I feel you need him removed from the family circle. You have had enough trouble with him. I know he doesn't plan to stay in school and that means incarceration. He doesn't need a year with kids more experienced in crime. I'm going to try to brainwash him into the army. The discipline there would be what he needs, and I sincerely feel he'd do okay with Uncle Sam."

Mr. Jackson succeeded. Bob went to take the army entrance exam, and a few days later the corporal in charge called to report his score. Since Bob was at a weekend retreat with the church youth group, I took the message. "Bob passed the test, Mrs. Nyberg, but barely. If he is sincere in wanting to get into the service, he'd better jump now. If he had to take the test again, he might not pass. It was too close."

When Bob returned, he telephoned Mr. Jackson to discuss the situation. They both went to talk with the recruiting officer. Bob was promised that if he got through boot camp without any problems, he could go into the Motor Vehicle Corps for training in driving and mechanics. He decided to enlist.

About this time another vocation change was in the wind for Don. This would mean a move south to a warmer climate. We decided to make the change. Don left for the new job while the boys and I remained behind to sell the house. On the day of Bob's induction we drove him to camp. A few weeks after we sold the house, the moving van arrived to load our belongings. We piled our car full and followed the van toward our new home. We were off on another adventure.

David had decided that if we were moving to California, he wanted to finish college there. He had been accepted even on short notice, so we were still to be a family of four—only a different four from the previous year. Bob was off on his new career with Uncle Sam, and we hoped this time we had the answer.

10
G.I. Bob

Bob's experiences at boot camp were moderately tranquil. He did complain about his old head injury because he claimed to be having terrible headaches. He wrote:

Mom cant you get a letter from the doc that fixed my hed it hurts all the time ok Bob

His words were, as usual, spelled phonetically and written in one long sentence. The message came through, however—he wanted out.

The letter I wrote back was short and simple:

Dear Bob,

You passed your physical. You must also remember the doctor said you'd have no trouble from your injury. You will have to stick it out, Bob. We're proud of you! Pray every day and ask Jesus to help you. He always will.

Love,

Mom and Dad

Other than falling and breaking his arm, Bob survived the rigors of boot camp.

Because we moved as he entered the service, Bob's first

two-week furlough was spent in our new town where he had no friends. Bob never wanted to go places with us before, but this time he went willingly because there was nothing else to do. We had a peaceful, pleasant time doing things together as a unified family.

While he was at home, Bob gave us the only compliment we ever received from him. "Mom, I never would have made it through boot camp if it hadn't been for you and Dad."

"Why do you say that?" I asked.

"It's because you were so tough when it came to disciplining. I hated it when I was at home, but if you hadn't been tough on me, I never could have taken it at camp. It was *really* tough. I didn't like their rules any better than yours, but I made it because I was used to it. A lot of guys went AWOL because they couldn't take orders."

Bob's next assignment would be at Ford Ord, California, for training in vehicle mechanics. He left by bus, excited to get back to his friends. We were on a "high" period and felt it was God who wanted Bob in the army, not just his probation officer and his family.

Each stage in Bob's life caused us to do a great deal of self-evaluation. *Have we been too strict? Not strict enough? It is so easy to let anger and frustration control emotions. Have we kept a balance of love and discipline?*

Don and I knew we made mistakes and would continue to make them. It is only God who never makes errors. We were thankful we had the strength of his love to uphold us in times of trial. We believed he was in control, molding both our positive training and our faults into his own plan for Bob. We prayed that the Holy Spirit would always be with our son.

At the climax of his special training Bob was assigned to overseas duty in Germany. My parents were vacationing with us, and we drove up the California coastline to visit Bob at Ford Ord before he shipped out. The army base is located near Monterey, and we settled into a motel in that picturesque city. Its lush green countryside and magnificent Mission gave me a sense of history.

Bob, accompanied by a friend, spent part of his free time with us. This friend, clean-cut and polite, appeared to be the kind we wished Bob would find. During our visit Bob told us, "I couldn't read some of the training manuals, but teachers helped and I passed all the tests."

"I'm grateful you had officers willing to help. That was God at work for you," I replied. "Don't ever forget all he gives you each day, Bob."

It was with mixed emotions that we said good-by as Bob embarked on his first overseas tour of duty. Letters from Germany came sporadically. They were short and poorly written. Bob reported army life was great. He was driving the vehicles more than working on them.

After Bob had been in Germany about eight months, we received a startling letter. Our eighteen-year-old wrote:

Hi Mom and Dad Just wantd you to no I am engag Her nam is Sarah no youll lik her love Bob

Following an exchange of several letters, we learned a few particulars. Sarah was reportedly the daughter of an army officer stationed at the same base. Bob was excited that she had chosen him to fall in love with over all the other available boys. He had bought her a small diamond at the PX and assured us they were not considering marriage for a long time.

Bob proposed to every girl he dated a few times. In love with love, Bob wanted a girl for a possession. Thankfully, every girl so far had been intelligent enough to recognize that he wasn't ready for marriage. Now we wondered.

When Bob left to go overseas, we encouraged him to have a small allotment sent home to be banked. This would provide him with money when he returned. He had never been able to save, and we encouraged this method. He agreed. Each month we received and dutifully deposited his allotment check.

Before too many months, however, he started writing and asking for it back. It was always an emergency or the need to buy something that was a "super" bargain. We sent it to him as requested for a time, but when he began asking for an advance on what had not as yet arrived, we said, "No!" Bob pouted through the mails, but I explained, "When you get home, Bob, you'll be glad we made you save. Now that you are engaged, you need to save even more seriously."

I feared he would stop the allotment. He asked for money from his savings so often that by the time we decided to refuse, there was little left. Just before returning stateside he wrote us one last letter begging for his cash. We ignored the request.

11
Vietnam

After his year in Germany Bob re-enlisted. He arrived home broke and announced, "I've volunteered to go to Vietnam!"

What a greeting! No mother wants her son in the midst of a war—but that wasn't the only thing that alarmed both Don and me. We heard about the rampant use of drugs among servicemen in Vietnam, and the idea that Bob would face that kind of temptation dismayed us. His compulsion for instant self-gratification would doubtless override any question of right or wrong. We knew he was being thrust into two kinds of action.

"Have you ever used drugs?" I asked Bob while he sat watching me prepare dinner.

"I tried marijuana," he replied, "but it didn't turn me on."

Bob has many allergies to medication. Please God, use that to keep him from becoming caught up in the drug scene.

But future worries were not our only concern. We wondered about his finances. When Bob reenlisted, he had received $365. He was vague about where the money went and silent as to the disposition of his belongings. He had used his allotment savings to buy many items, including cameras, tape decks, and a stereo. He had told us the bargains were "too good to pass up." But it bothered us that he returned home with only his clothing.

My parents had retired during Bob's year in Germany and

moved to California to enjoy the warmer weather. Bob liked their company and spent time with them while on furlough. He told his grandfather that he had played a lot of poker overseas, and Dad said to him, "Come on, Bob, let's play. It's been a long time since I've played poker. Never played much and I wasn't good, but I'll give it a try."

After a few games Dad reported, "I bet I know where his money went. Bob said he played for pretty high stakes. He told me he'd won most of the time, but there is no way he could have. I'm no poker player, but I won almost every game. He probably lost his cameras and stuff the same way. There are sharp poker players in the service. They'll let a person win just enough to get him hooked and then wipe him out."

When we asked Bob about the cameras, he mentioned "hocking a few items" while in the service. He has continued to use that system of raising cash in civilian life, following his childhood pattern of never becoming attached to any possession. He used to sell his belongings to friend or foe whenever he tired of them.

I recall when he worked valiantly to earn ten dollars to buy a wet-suit. We had no ocean nearby, but we could not talk him out of his desire. After finally acquiring the suit, he soon lost interest and sold it to another boy for one dollar. "Hard come, easy go" seemed to be his motto. Apparently it had not changed.

While Bob was home on furlough, I also attempted to learn more about our possible daughter-in-law. He said, "Sarah is still in Germany, but she will be coming back to the States soon. I won't see her again until I get back from Vietnam." This fact didn't seem to bother him, and we wondered if his short attention span was dissolving his engagement plans, too. While at home, he dated every available girl. He had saved $150 by our forced savings plan, and now he seemed determined to spend every cent as fast as he could. Many nights he didn't return home until dawn. This disturbed us, but he was now an adult living away from home. He was really only with us for a visit.

We kept silent about our feelings, but I did let him know

how I felt about his infidelity to Sarah. "Bob, if you're engaged, you have no business dating other girls. It isn't fair to Sarah."

"Mom, don't worry. Sarah and I have an agreement. She is dating and so am I until I get back from Vietnam."

This arrangement was not according to our beliefs, but we chose not to interfere with *their* decision . . . *if* it were a double decision. It is a test for parents in such situations to leave their children in the Lord's hands. Don and I kept reminding ourselves to stay out of his plans. God was all Bob needed.

On the last day of his leave Ann, a sixteen-year-old neighborhood girl, stopped at the house to see Bob on her way to school. I watched her say good-by to him and shuddered at the passion she threw at him. He told Donny before he left what an "easy" date she was. Every boy in the neighborhood had bragged to David about their dates with her and tried to talk him into taking her out, but David wasn't interested. Bob, on the other hand, was proud he was one of the boys who had been out with her.

Now our soldier boy was on his way to war. He left, telling us, "I'll probably never see you again."

"Bob, you've been through so many close calls with your neurosurgery and millions of accidents that you'll get through this without a mark. Just you see if I'm not right," Don said in his final words of encouragement. Despite all the heartaches Bob had brought into our lives, it was a chilling experience for us to send our son off to Vietnam.

Shortly after Bob's departure, we received a letter from Sarah, postmarked "New York City." Her spelling and writing ability matched Bob's, and the content of her letter left me numb. We had felt so encouraged with Bob's attitude and personality changes. He had survived almost two years in the army without serious trouble, but now we discovered he was still being totally untruthful.

Sarah's letter told how happy she was to be becoming a part of our family. To introduce herself, she explained that she had two older and two younger brothers and that her father was a factory worker.

She had never traveled beyond New York and was thrilled when Bob had sent her a diamond ring. They had been writing for a long time, she told us, and their friendship had simply grown into "love." She added that she was in no hurry to get married, but wished Bob had received a furlough before going to Vietnam. She wanted so badly to see him.

We were flattened. Her story was so completely different from what Bob had told us. *Why*, we wondered, *had he felt it necessary to fabricate such a story?* He apparently had no desire to meet her in person, but why all the lies? We felt we understood our son even less than before. Sarah concluded her letter by asking me to write her because she wanted to get to know the family.

One of the psychiatrists we previously consulted said, "Bob lives in a dream world so much of the time that he doesn't know where fantasy and reality end or come together." Was this still true?

I quickly wrote a letter to Bob:

Dear Bob,

Now I want you to read every word of this letter! It is *important!* You have put me on the spot. Sarah wrote. I won't waste time telling you all she said because you know all about her. We now know that she has never been out of the United States. Her father works in a factory in New York.

Now, Private Nyberg, what do I write back? Do I tell her how surprised I was to learn you have never even seen her? And how sorry we are that you wouldn't stop to see her on the furlough you told her you wouldn't have? Do I lie to her and tell her you told us her true story? (You know I won't do that!) I don't want to tell her we didn't know her story, either. I don't want to mention that you just spent two weeks with us enroute to Vietnam. It is going to be a difficult letter to write.

What I want from you is the truth from start to finish so I won't get caught saying something that is wrong. We thought you had finally grown up and were being honest. Now I have to know the facts. Where did you meet her? Or find out about

her? Will you please tell all immediately!
Love, Mom and Dad

We received a return letter in record time. Bob wrote:

Dear Mom and Dad I don't no why I told you that story I start riting to her got her name from a friend and it just got so we new we were in love she is pretty and rites every day and I rite her to and Im sorry I lide to you I was afrad to see her wen I was hom she mit not love me plees dont tell her you didnt no where she lived ok with love your son Bob.

Bob had spent much of his life being angry with us, but when he was in trouble he always appealed to us for help.

I sat down and composed a letter to Sarah, telling her now nice it had been to hear from her and that we enjoyed hearing about her family. I mentioned that Bob seldom wrote to us and so we had not heard too much about her (which was true). I also explained that I was not a dependable letter writer but would be happy to correspond sporadically. I also introduced her to the other members of our family.

Several months later we received a letter from Sarah stating that she was concerned about Bob. He had been writing regularly, but now it had been months since she had received a letter. Her letters had not been returned, and she was worried.

I wrote Bob, asking him to *please* write Sarah because she was concerned about his safety. I told him we knew he was busy, but we didn't want to have to cover his thoughlessness.

His answer left us with a new and decidedly different problem. Bob announced that he no longer intended to write to Sarah. He had married a Vietnamese girl and was teaching her English so she could come to America and live with us until he returned from Vietnam. He asked our help in filling out the necessary papers.

Our prayers that night were filled with petitions. What should we do about this new enigma? Bob always managed to outdo himself—eight thousand miles away and still creating frustrations! His new request involved too many complications. We would have no difficulty loving a Vietnamese daughter-in-law, but what about Sarah? Bob hadn't even had the courtesy to write a "Dear Jane" letter. How long would this marriage last? How soon would his ardor cool? Would we end with a Vietnamese girl as our responsibility, and perhaps a baby as well? What next? All these and many other questins tumbled through our minds that day and long into the night.

The following morning I called the nearest service base requesting an appointment with the chaplain. It was confirmed for two days later, and so we spent two days torturously mulling over Bob's situation. With Bob's letter in hand I went to the appointment. I wanted the chaplain to see that this nineteen-year-old was neither emotionally nor mentally capable of supporting a family.

The chaplain's immediate statement was, "Mrs. Nyberg, you must not help your son bring this girl home. As terrible as conditions are there, she is better off with her own people. If your son is as unstable as you say, and his letter appears, he would not stay with her very long after she arrived here. Then either you and your husband or the Welfare Department would have another family to support. With the language and cultural differences, she would be lost and unhappy. Her place is right where she is.

"I suggest you write to Bob's chaplain," he continued. "I'll get you his name. Tell him what I've said and that I told you to write. You might suggest you'd rather not have Bob know you've written. Bob needs counseling, and so does this girl. The chaplain will help them both and know best how to handle the situation. This happens many times over there.

"That's one reason why the army has made it so difficult to get Vietnamese wives back to the United States," the chaplain explained. "If a man is not intelligent enough to complete the necessary forms, the army knows he will be unable to cope with the problems of a wife of a different culture, race, and religion in America.

"Write to Bob" he concluded. "Tell him what you have

told me about your ability to love her completely if he brings her home, but that you will not be able to help him do it. That is his responsibility as an adult, one who thinks himself old enough to be married. He will not get her here; I can guarantee that as a fact."

I felt both relief and worry after my visit with the chaplain. I knew he was right, but what about the baby that was possibly on the way? The chaplain had agreed this was a certainty. What kind of future lay ahead for a little baby? We had gone for advice, and Don convinced me that it was foolish for us not to heed it.

I wrote the chaplain and Bob as he suggested, and I told the chaplain that I would not expect a reply. We knew he was too busy for letter writing, but we expressed our thanks for the help he would be giving our son. We took courage in knowing that although Bob appeared to be oblivious to God's presence, our Lord was graciously with him. The fact that Jesus was the only one to whom we could turn reinforced us.

Several weeks later Bob wrote a pleasant letter stating that he wasn't really married. He had just made up that story.

12
Returning Warrior

When Bob's tour ended, he was not anxious to return home. Stationed miles from the front lines, he had enjoyed working on and driving the vehicles and possibly spending his free time with his "wife." He wrote:

Som guys got shot not me I was luky love Bob.

However, his tour overseas was completed, and now he had to return to the States. After his furlough he would be stationed in Texas until his enlistment expired. He arrived home as cheery as if he'd been on a picnic, and the lazy days passed quickly. I cooked all Bob's favorite foods. It was another happy family time.

Returning from the mailbox one afternoon, I called to Bob. "Here's a letter from Sarah."

"Golly," he exclaimed after he opened the letter, "she wants me to visit her. What should I do?"

"Bob, I honestly think you owe it to both of you to at least see each other. Then you can decide whether or not to continue your engagement or break it off. Without having ever seen one another, it's difficult to know what to do."

"Maybe I should go this week, then."

"If you decide to go, it would be more sensible to go to

New York at the end of your leave and go directly from there to Texas. It would be less expensive, and you don't have too much money to spend."

"I don't want to be there very long because I don't know them or anything. Maybe I'll go for a couple of days before Texas."

Bob left for Texas via New York. When he arrived at camp, he informed us that the engagement was off. Sarah, he wrote, had lost the ring anyhow, and she just wasn't his type.

We wrote back to assure him that the right girl would come along and not to be too anxious to take on the responsibilities of marriage. We felt the government was right to make it difficult for servicemen to bring home Vietnamese wives, but we hoped it would not encourage Bob to start a pattern of walking away from further relationships and responsibilities.

A week later, another letter arrived from Bob:

Dear Mom and Dad Sarah is coming to see me we are in love I am excited
Love Bob

Several days later Don was at home when the telephone rang. It was long distance from Texas. One of Bob's superior officers asked, "Will you give permission for Bob and Sarah to be married? I suggest you do so, because they'll probably find a way to marry regardless."

Don gave his consent. I agreed that it was the only thing to do. We presumed they had married immediately and prayed the marriage would be a good one. Sarah had apparently gone to Texas with marriage in mind. She had taken all her belongings with her, and she and Bob had set up housekeeping in a small, rented trailer near the base.

Before long, numerous reverse-charge telephone calls started coming to California. "Mom, can you send us some money? We can't make it on my pay." Or, "Can you send me my sleeping bag and guitar?"

Each time it was for something they wanted us to do for

them. We tried to explain that they could write for the price of a stamp. "Bob," I said as I again accepted a call, "this is the last time I will accept charges."

"But, Mom, we have tried to get a telephone, but they don't have any. We can't use a friend's phone for long-distance calls."

"No, but you could call from a pay phone or do as we do—write letters. Nothing you call about is so important it couldn't be handled in a letter. So from now on that's the rule. We won't accept reverse charges."

Bob hung up in a huff without even saying why he had called that time, but he made another call several weeks later. I hesitated to accept the charges and heard Bob tell the operator, "She's just got to accept."

There was panic in his voice, so I said, "Yes."

"I'm in trouble. I caught a guy from the trailer park bothering Sarah, and I hit him. He called the cops, and I was arrested. I need the money for a lawyer to keep me out of jail."

"Won't the army help you?"

"No, because it happened while I was off duty and off base."

The story sounded suspicious, but Don and I had tried not to doubt everything Bob said. He had lied so often through the years. *God, what should I answer this time?* I silently prayed. Don wasn't at home; there was no one to help me decide. "Okay," I replied, "but this is strictly a loan, and it must be paid back. It is your problem, and there is no reason for us to have to bail you out. Remember, it is a loan!"

"Gee, thanks, Mom. I knew you wouldn't let us down. I'll pay it back right away, I promise."

I sighed as I replaced the receiver. That promise had been given so many times before and immediately dismissed from his mind. Perhaps he was growing up and this time would be different.

We wired the funds and heard nothing. After several letters from us asking what had happened, Bob called to report that Sarah had left him and gone home to her parents.

"What about the lawsuit?" we asked. "Is that why she left?"

"Oh, everything is okay about that—no problem," he flippantly replied. We knew at once that we had been conned again. At that time we had no idea how Bob had spent our funds. I realized I should have asked for the attorney's name so I could have mailed the check directly to him, but I hadn't thought of it in time. Now our money was gone someplace, but certainly not to a lawyer.

The next call came from New York. "I'm in New York," Bob reported. "I've enlisted to go back to Vietnam, so I have two weeks' leave. I came here to see Sarah. Guess what—she's pregnant!"

Bob knew how much we loved babies, and I could sense his manipulative mind whirling. He would use this little addition to their family to maneuver us. We felt saddened because we knew neither of them were ready for parenthood.

During Bob's next call he announced, "We're coming in on the 8:10 plane tomorrow morning. Sarah wants to meet you, and I want her to see you guys. I'll leave from there next week for Vietnam. Mom, can Sarah stay with you while I'm gone? It would be so much fun for you when the baby comes. I'd feel safer if she were with you."

"Sorry, Bob, but the answer to that request has to be no," I stated. Don chorused the same thing from the extension phone. "While you are away, her place is with her parents. She wouldn't have any friends here, and she needs her mother at this time."

He didn't argue, but we knew that he wanted to. "We'll meet your plane in the morning and are looking forward to meeting Sarah. See you tomorrow," Don said.

Bob and Sarah arrived all bubbly and smiling like newlyweds. This was the first meeting of the Nyberg family with the new Mrs. Nyberg. She was tall and willowy with beautiful red hair. Her pregnancy didn't show at all. She seemed very quiet and sweet.

At this time I was employed full-time by the county. David had finished college. Established in a good position, he was working his way up the corporate ladder. He had his own apartment, but he often ate with us. Donny, who was in college and working part-time, was in and out of the house at all hours. Bob and Sarah settled in like part of the family. They toured all the local sightseeing attractions while we were off to work and lazed around the pool in their "at home" time.

When I arrived home from work, they were usually stretched out in front of the television set watching cowboys and cartoons. Bob had always loved the "shoot 'em out" cowboy pictures. We found we had to forbid them when he was a youngster because they overexcited him. Now he was happy watching what he enjoyed.

One day when I came home from work and walked through the kitchen, I literally stuck to the floor. "What on earth is on this floor?" I asked.

"Oh," Bob laughed, "we made lemonade and spilled the whole pitcher."

"Didn't you even try to clean it up?"

"We sopped it up with paper towels," he replied.

I changed my clothes, got out my pail, and scrubbed the kitchen floor before starting to prepare dinner. *This is the girl Bob wanted us to keep while he was overseas!* I thought. We said nothing because we wanted their visit to be pleasant, but she never volunteered to help during their entire stay. We were certainly relieved that we had said "no" to a permanent visit.

The day before their departure Bob announced they had no money to purchase Sarah's ticket home or get him to his point of embarkation.

"Bob, we recently lent you $300 that you seem to have forgotten about. There will be no more money from us. You'd better get on the telephone and call Sarah's parents for money for her ticket."

"But there isn't time!"

"Yes there is. They can do one of two things—either buy her a ticket there that she can pick up at the airport or wire the money. We're not going to hand out any more cash."

Bob made the telephone call and obtained a ticket for

Sarah. We had to pay for Bob's ticket, though, since Sarah's parents couldn't be expected to furnish that. Her flight left first, and we had an hour to chat until Bob's departure.

"Bob, let's have some straight answers to a couple of questions. That $300—what really happened to it? It did *not* go to any lawyer. Were you even in any trouble? Let's have the truth."

"Well," he hesitated, "I did threaten to hit the guy because he was always bothering Sarah. But we thought it was the only way to get the money. Sarah was mad at me because I volunteered to go back to Vietnam. She wanted to go home right away, and the money bought her a ticket."

"Okay, that's part of it. A one-way ticket from Texas to New York doesn't cost $300. Where did the rest go?"

"I felt bad and I didn't want to lose her, so I got an emergency leave and flew to New York to try to make up. I also bought her a pedigreed poodle. It helped her decide to stay married to me. And then she found out, too, that she was pregnant. So we made up."

Don and I looked at each other and again read each other's mind. *A precious baby, possibly a little Bob.* There was nothing we as parents could do to help Bob and Sarah, but it was difficult to keep out of God's way and let him be in complete control. Every day we prayed for the ability to let them be independent adults.

13
Matrimonial Mayhem

The first telephone bill we received after Bob and Sarah's visit almost caused a coronary. Sarah had called her parents every day for long, chatty visits at daytime rates. We had never had such an immense bill—one hundred and fifteen dollars. Bob and Sarah were starting marriage with no knowledge of finances and a baby on the way. It was frightening!

Shortly after Bob returned to Vietnam, letters began arriving. We were bombarded from both sides. Sarah wrote that Bob wasn't sending her any allotment; Bob wrote that he had sent all his pay to Sarah and needed money. We were in the middle, attempting to keep our sanity while saying no to requests for money from both directions.

Then Sarah wrote and asked if she could come to live with us. She claimed her mother was working her like a slave. We again said "no!"

Bob's letters were filled with distrust of Sarah. He accused her of "chasing on him" and said he'd feel better if we'd let her live with us.

On this tour of duty Bob was stationed near the center of action. We didn't want him to worry about his wife and attempted to reassure him without changing our decision about where Sarah should live. I answered his letter:

Bob, if Sarah is chasing on you in New York, she'll chase

on you if she were with us. I can't sit home and keep track of her. That isn't the answer. Frankly, I can't imagine a girl who is seven months pregnant doing much chasing. I think you are making up things to worry about. God is in charge—remember!

The Red Cross informed Bob when Sarah entered the hospital and kept him updated until Bob Junior arrived. Bob was ecstatic about being a daddy, and according to Sarah's reports their strong, healthy son was an exact replica of Bob.

Soon Bob's correspondence reported letters from Sarah's mother saying that Sarah was not being a good mother. According to him, she was not caring for the baby and was chasing around. We wrote Bob, telling him to await judgment until he got home. His tour of duty was almost over. When he returned he could see what was happening. Sarah's father assured Bob that he could help him get work at the factory where he was employed. Bob and Sarah planned to remain in New York.

A few weeks before Bob was to come home he wrote to suggest that Bobby and Sarah fly to California and be with us to meet him when he got back. Since I was already committed to be a delegate at a church conference in the East, I suggested that Bob meet Sarah in New York. Don and I would meet them there at the end of my conference.

They both agreed, and the new plans went into effect.

Then Bob wrote his final request:

I need $400 rite away I got to hav it befor I com hom
Love Bob

"No way!" we answered.

We next heard from Sarah, who wrote to tell us that Bob was mad at us. He was flying directly to New York and didn't ever want to see us again. We wrote back:

I'm sorry, Sarah, but don't worry about Bob being mad. This happens all the time. He'll get over it. Dad and I will go ahead with our original plans. When my conference is over, I'll fly to meet Don at his family's home, where we'll spend two weeks. Then we'll both go home. Bob will get over it. He just can't adjust to being told "no."

My worry and concern over Bob and his young family were more than I could handle with the heavy responsibilities of my job, so I had requested a leave of absence. I did not at that time plan to return to work, but I left the door open in case I changed my mind.

I departed for my conference and for four days was out of touch with my family and the world. My days were packed full of inspiration and the knowledge that God is with us always, especially in times of distress with our kids. On the last of the conference I felt an urgency to check up on my family. I called home, and Mom answered. Don had already left for the Midwest where I would meet him.

"We have been having a flurry of calls between New York and California," Mom said. "Bob wants to bring Bobby home. Don asked him who would take care of Bobby, and Bob's reply was—Mom. Don then informed him that you had to go back to work." (My future was sealed.)

"And all this time I've been peacefully enjoying my conference," I remarked.

"We're all so glad you had this opportunity to be away from the mess."

"What brought it all on, Mom? Last I knew Bob never wanted to see or hear from us."

"It seems he and Sarah aren't going to stay together, and Bob wants to come home with the baby."

"Doesn't Sarah object to his wanting the baby?"

"That part hasn't been investigated. Don is so upset to think that they aren't even trying. But the next bit is unbelievable. When Don asked who Bob thought would take of Bobby with you at work, Bob said, 'Why can't Grandma?' Don really squelched that one. He told Bob that I was an old lady, half-blind, and that great-grandmothers weren't made to take care of babies. Dad and I have been chuckling over his handling of the situation, but he was right.

"We thought that had settled matters," Mom continued, "but then the calls began again. This time Don told Bob that if he and Sarah couldn't resolve their difficulties, they'd better place Bobby for adoption. Don reminded him that such a decision would put their baby in the same situation he had been in."

"Wow! I bet Don was glad to get away this morning."

"He was, and we were glad he could, but we've had a call since he left. When we told Bob his dad was gone, he wanted Uncle Joe's phone number. Don will be hearing more, I'm sure."

"Guess I'd better quit before I run up too big a bill. Sorry you've all had so much trouble, but I'm really glad I didn't know about it. It would have ruined my time here. Say 'hi' to everyone, and we'll see you in a couple of weeks."

In the meantime Sarah knew my plans to arrive in New York to change planes for the Midwest. She and Bob decided to chance finding me at the airport. If my flight out hadn't been delayed, I would have missed them. As it turned out, we met in the terminal. It was the only time I ever saw Bobby Junior. He looked so much like Bob it was unbelievable. Bob may have heard rumors about Sarah's infidelity, but there was no question in my mind that this son was really his.

"Sarah," I asked, "with such a beautiful baby, why don't you want to work at your marriage? Surely he alone is worth the effort?"

"Oh, I've already decided to stay married," she replied. She gave no further explanation of the trouble, and I didn't press for information.

My plane was announced on the intercom. As I settled into my seat, I breathed a sigh of relief. Perhaps this little family would not be fractured after all. My prayer was, "Please, God, don't allow these kids to use this innocent baby as a pawn in their unstable marriage."

14
Incest

After the aura surrounding my conference experiences, my meeting with Bob and Sarah catapulted me back to reality. When Don met me at the airport, I was on the verge of tears. It was wonderful to be held in his strong, supportive arms.

We knew that once we let the appeal of young Bobby capture our hearts, we would be unable to let go. Bob knew our weakness—we couldn't resist a baby. Although our two weeks with Don's family were meant to give us rest and relaxation, Bob continued to bombard us with calls, pleading with us to let him come home with Bobby. I was so emotionally torn I couldn't digest my food and became ill.

The thunderbolt came with Bob's final call from New York. "Mom," Bob's voice rushed at me across the miles of telephone lines "Sarah insists on a divorce."

"We've been through this before, Bob," I said, my voice quivering. "You're a grown man with a wife and son. You can't just move in and out of our home at will. You can go back to California, but not to live with us. We always said that when you married, you would be on your own."

"But you don't understand. Sarah is pregnant again, and she doesn't want me or Bobby anymore."

I was speechless. Don, on the extension phone, also made no reply. When I was finally able to talk, I said, "Let me talk to

Sarah. I want to hear what she has to say."

"Hi," came Sarah's voice.

"Is what Bob tells me true? That you are pregnant with someone else's child and no longer want to remain married to Bob?"

"Yes," she replied.

"Do you want to marry the father of this child?"

"Didn't Bob tell you?"

"Tell me what?"

"I can't marry the father."

"Then why not stay married to Bob?"

"Didn't he tell you who the father is?"

"No." This time the one word answer was mine.

"It's my brother."

Dead silence. I could hear Don's heart beating as he, too, felt the impact of those words. *Incest! Do those kids know what they are talking about?* "Sarah, may I speak to your mother?" I asked.

"Sure, I'll call her."

When her mother came on the line, I said, "Is what Sarah tells me true?"

"I guess so," she replied. "I have gone to try to get counseling help for the kids. We don't know what to do."

"Well, I think Bob had better stay there and get in on any professional help available. We've already told him we cannot raise Bobby for him. They will have to place him for adoption if they can't make a go of it."

"We'll never allow that," she replied. "We'll raise Bobby if necessary."

"Will you put Bob back on the line, please?" I asked again.

When Bob came back on the phone, I said, "Bob, your dad and I will leave tomorrow for home if we can get reservations. We'll investigate foster home care for Bobby, but you stick right there until you hear from us. It will be several days. Sarah's mother is getting professional help for you all. Please go. We'll be in touch in a few days."

We were able to get reservations on the midnight flight the

next day. Cutting our vacation short, we left for home. On the airplane I reviewed the conference in my mind, clinging to the peace I had received there. One passage, Jeremiah 29:11, had rescued me from despair: "For I know the plans I have for you, says the Lord. They are plans for good and not for evil, to give you a future and a hope."

Donny met the plane, and we arrived at our house in the middle of the night, exhausted. The following day was Sunday, and we approached our minister after the service. "Dr. Brown, we have an extremely serious problem that we need expert advice on."

"I can see you at 10:00 tomorrow morning if that's convenient," he replied. "It's my day off, but I'd be happy to come in."

When I entered his office the next day, I tried to keep my emotions controlled. I gave him a capsule description of our problems with Bob and then poured out his latest catastrophe.

"Dorothea," he said, stretching his hands out to their full width and placing them with fingertips touching his desk, "I can tell you exactly what to do, but it is up to you whether or not you will take my advice. Don't touch that baby with a ten-foot pole—no, a twenty-foot pole. You and Don have been through enough trying to make Bob into a decent, law-abiding citizen. You have had enough problems with Bob. Don't even consider trying to raise his son."

Later, Don and I discussed what we should do. Ultimately, we decided to heed the advice we had sought. We telephoned Bob that evening to tell him our decision. "Bob, we will welcome you home if you want to come, but we can't take Bobby. There is no one here to care for him while you work. An infant's place is with his mother."

"Oh, that's okay," he glibly replied. "I don't want to come home. We're going to stay married. We bought a car today, and I have a job where Sarah's dad works." He was as happy as a kid with a new toy. We even mentally questioned the truth of Sarah's pregnancy. At this point we didn't know what to think and tried to return to our pattern of life by putting Bob's problems behind us.

15
Gone!

Three months later another telephone call came. "Mom, please send me a ticket to come home. Sarah has locked me out of our apartment. I have been sleeping in my car, and I want to come home."

"What about your job and the car? When do you get paid next?"

"Well, the car isn't worth as much as we owe on it, and my boss says he'll mail my paycheck to your address. He thinks I should leave Sarah, too. It's cold here sleeping in the car. I've had it with her!"

We wired him a ticket, and he arrived smelling as if he hadn't taken a bath in a month. "Sarah didn't want me," he told us, "because my hospitalization insurance at work wouldn't cover the cost of the new baby's delivery. If I wasn't around, she'd be eligible for welfare."

"That's dishonest, Bob."

"I know, but try to tell her anything. I told her I was willing to accept the new baby, and Mom, I just have to get Bobby away from her."

"Bob, you can go in and talk to our lawyer about it, but I cannot take care of Bobby for you."

"Okay, but I'll get a job and then I can pay someone to take care of him. I'd be home every night to be with him after work."

"Bob, I wish I could believe that. I just know I'd be left with him most of the time, and I'm too old and too tired to start raising another child."

"Couldn't we try?"

"We'll talk to our attorney and then abide by his decision. What did you do with your car? Did you notify the bank you were turning it back to them?"

"Yes, I took it to them, and a friend from work drove me to the airport."

A few days later Sarah called and asked where Bob had left the car. The finance company was looking for it because a payment was past due. Bob finally admitted he had left it in a parking lot at the airport.

"When we told you that you could come home, the one stipulation was that we would demand honesty at all times." Don stared intently at Bob. "The past was to be forgiven and forgotten, but no more lying would be tolerated. Now here we are back in your old routine. Bob, why do you lie?"

"I don't know. I just didn't want to tell you. I had to get to the airport, and the company will get their old car. It's no sweat! What does it matter?"

We helped Bob find a steady job, got him outfitted in some clothes, and located an old clunker for transportation to and from work. Everything looked smooth for the moment, and Bob decided to talk to our lawyer.

"Bob, we'll make an appointment for you to talk to our attorney," Don said, "but you must follow whatever advice he gives you. There are too many legal angles in trying to get custody of a child for anyone to do anything without legal advice. And remember, there is still the problem of who will care for him."

When Bob went to the appointment, the lawyer advised, "Bob, no court will award a father custody over a mother if she wants the child. Even a murder rap might not sway a judge. They just think 'mother.'" Bob returned home dejected.

Every morning each of us left for our various occupations

—Don to his, me to mine, Bob to his, and Donny to college. Suppertime was pleasant, with all of us sharing our day's happenings. Bob would be quiet at times and when asked what the trouble was, he's shake his head and say, "Oh, I miss Bobby."

But soon he was out every night, getting home extremely late. Then it would be hard to get him moving in the morning. One day he announced, "I quit my job today."

"Why, Bob?" we asked.

"Oh, there wasn't any future there." He had been working as an orderly at a hospital. He had been promoted to kitchen helper, and the cook wanted to train him to be a chef. Bob had always done well in his culinary attempts and enjoyed puttering in the kitchen. All had appeared to be going well.

"What's the new job?" we continued questioning.

He hesitated and then replied, "I'm a bouncer in a bar."

One Saturday he brought home a young girl with a baby. "Mom, this is Marilyn. She works with me, and I'm trying to help her. We both have the night off and want you to take care of the baby while we go out."

"Sorry," I said, "but we have plans for tonight."

Bob's face became flushed, but he held off his anger until the next morning when he started a tirade. I explained, "This is the reason I don't want Bobby here. I would be left with him far too often while you chase. You're still a married man and have no business going our with any girls. Where is this girl's husband?"

"She doesn't have one and never did. Her kid is illegitimate."

The bar where he worked turned out to be of the topless variety. It was raided and closed, and Bob was once again unemployed. Then one day we came home to find him gone, along with everything he owned. We didn't hear from him for weeks. We were never certain where he might be. Friends of Donny and Dave reported having seen him in bars, but how he supported himself we didn't know. Today he is vague when asked about these periods.

Months later the telephone rang. The operator said, "I

have a person-to-person call for Mr. or Mrs. Nyberg.

"This is Mrs. Nyberg," I replied.

"Mrs. Nyberg," a strange voice said, "you don't know me, but Bob arrived at my home with our son last night. They were both tired and dirty. He's had a good night's sleep, some food, a bath, and wants to go home. He is hurt, and we thought you might want to send him plane fare. We live in Texas."

"How serious is his injury?"

"Not too bad, but he's limping."

"Well, my husband and I have talked at length about what to do in this type of situation. Don isn't home, but we decided if our wandering son called for fare home again, we'd say no. I think I'd better stick with that decision. Send him to the county hospital if he needs medical aid, but he'll have to take care of himself. We have had it."

"I know what you mean. We've been through this too. I still felt I had to call."

Our pastor's wife from a previous church said to me one day, "Dorothea, you have simply got to lock that boy out. Change the key if necessary. He is not the prodigal son. The prodigal son came home asking nothing; Bob only comes home when he wants something. You have it mixed up. You've got to face the fact that the best thing for Bob is to be forced to stand on his own two feet. As long as you and Don are available and willing to help him out, he'll disappear and reappear at his whim." I held on to that advice while waiting for Don to get home and reassure me I had done the right thing.

Two days later Bob rang our doorbell, walking as normally as ever. He wanted his astrology book, one of the fads he had become interested in during his wanderings. We agreed to let him stay until he got himself together, but this "getting himself together" was beginning to wear on us all. He located a job quickly, as usual. His problem was keeping jobs. He didn't necessarily get fired; more often he simply quit because he tired of working.

We soon discovered he was again working at the topless bar, much to our displeasure. It had reopened, and he had been rehired. For transportation he used another junker that we purchased for him. We secured insurance coverage and requested his first paycheck be turned over to us. We gave him spending money and the remainder paid for the car. His next check was to be handled in the same manner to pay for the insurance. Then he would be on his own with his paychecks. He agreed to this arrangement.

The day of his second paycheck Donny came home from college early because of a cancelled class. He was upstairs changing to go to work when he heard Bob come in. Bob went to his room and then headed downstairs and outside. After a repeat of this performance Donny went to see what was going on. Bob was packing all his belongings into his car.

"What are you up to now?" Donny asked.

"I'm leaving," Bob replied.

"You're nuts!" Donny said.

"Maybe you like it here, but I can't stand living at home. I'm getting out of here!"

"Bob, Mom and Dad are good enough to take you in when you're down and out. They deserve the courtesy of being told that you are planning to move out."

"Well, you can tell them for me. I can't stand it here!"

"I'll tell them all right. And next time you ask to move back in, I'll tell them to tell you to get lost!"

Bob turned away without answering, got into his car, revved up the engine, and turned the corner with a squeal of his tires that could be heard for blocks. "I wish a cop were around," Donny muttered to himself.

Several weeks later a neighboring car dealer called asking for Bob. "We don't know where he is," I said. "He doesn't live here anymore."

"He bought a car from us, and his next payment is past due."

"When he left home, he had a car that was fully paid for. What kind of a car did you sell him?"

"He traded a Volkswagen in on a Firebird."

"I don't know what you can do about it. You got a reliable

little car on the deal. We aren't responsible for his debts."

"Okay, we'll just put out a pickup notice on the car with the police. They'll find it. Thanks anyway."

Sometime later while at work I received a call from the receptionist. "A young man is here asking to see you. He says he's your son Bob."

I went out to the waiting room and motioned for Bob to follow me to an interviewing booth. "What can I do for you?"

"Will you help me fill out papers to reenlist?"

"Yes, I will. I think that's an excellent idea. You were in no trouble when you were in the service. It might help you settle down."

We set to work filling out the necessary papers. He could not do it alone. My only disappointment was that he was trying to enter the Marine Corps. I feared he would not make it there.

"Why the Marines this time, Bob?"

"Oh, I know a bunch of guys in there, and I thought it would be better than the army again."

He later told us he had been living at a Marine base for more than two months. He had his hair cut short and went in and out with his servicemen friends. They got bedding for him from the supply room, and he just walked into the mess hall with them. He claimed he was not the only one doing it.

Several weeks later he called to report he had not made it. He was extremely disappointed and wondered why. "Give me the name of the recruiting officer, and I'll call and see if I can find out why."

"We sent for his army records," the officer explained to me. "He had no bad marks, but he had been in for four years and only made it to PFC. Although he is separated from his wife, he is married with a child, so he would be paid for them, too. Frankly, because of the salary increase, we can be choosy."

"Thank you," I replied. "I can understand how those facts would affect his application."

Bob was upset. He never liked being told no and reacted by disappearing again. While he was gone, we received a letter from Sarah wanting to know where Bob was. The new baby, another boy, had been born, but he had multiple physical defects and had been hospitalized for the first three months of his life. Soon after she brought him home, he was found dead in his crib. The police had then arrested her for murder.

16
Unattainable Reconciliation

When we next heard from Bob, we told him what Sarah had written to us. He immediately got in touch with her parents. When Sarah was arrested, Bobby was to be made a ward of the court; but Sarah's parents stepped in and assumed responsibility for Bobby. Now Bob was full of compassion for Bobby, the son he had wanted so badly but given up so easily. All he could talk about was going back to New York to help. We discouraged this move, believing that Sarah's family would not welcome his entering the situation at this time.

One day he telephoned and asked, "Mom, would you give me the money to go to New York?"

"Sorry, but no money from us is the rule. You have never paid anything back, and your credit is no good."

"Will you buy my stereo for the price of a bus ticket?"

"Where did you get the stereo? Is it paid for?"

"I've had it quite a while and, yes, it's paid for. Will you buy it?"

We wondered about the history of the stereo, but felt if it were "hot" it would be better if we bought it than for Bob to sell it elsewhere. "Yes, we'll buy it," we said, "if you are certain Sarah's parents will welcome you." He assured us that they wanted him to come.

We picked him up at the address where he and a Marine

buddy were living and took him to the bus depot. We purchased the ticket and saw him onto the bus with the admonition, "Bob, if you don't stay there, we don't want to hear from you until you are reestablished, have a place to live, and have a job. We are not going to help you start over again."

"I agree, really. I will stay there and stand behind Sarah through her trial and be a father to Bobby. I promise I won't ask you for anything again."

Ten days later we were out in the front yard visiting with neighbors when the telephone rang. I went in to answer it. "Mom!"

I interrupted him. "Bob, we told you we didn't want to hear from you if you had problems."

"I know, but this is an emergency. I am at the airport in Los Angeles. Will you come and get me?"

"I'll let you talk to your dad," I replied. I walked out the front door in a daze, burst into tears, and told Don, "I simply can't take any more. Bob is at L.A. International and wants us to come and get him."

Don went in to talk to him. "How come you're back?" he asked.

"Sarah's lawyer thought it would be better if I weren't there, so her parents gave me plane fare home. I haven't any place to stay."

"Sorry, Bob, but you know the agreement. If you went to New York, you were not going to come back home again. You'll have to use your thumb. You can get a night's lodging at the Salvation Army if you can't find a friend to bunk with. We've had it!" With a good-by, Don replaced the receiver and returned to the front yard. "I told him no. Relax. He'll make out; he always does. That charm will see him through."

Several months later Sarah wrote to me and asked if we could correspond. She was out on bail, claimed her innocence, and had been assured that her attorney would get her off. Her case was postponed and postponed and finally came to trial more than a year later. In the meantime her pediatrician, who had said that he would testify in her behalf, had moved to the

West Coast. Her attorney then advised her to plead guilty to a lesser charge. She did so and was sentenced to fourteen years. She was shocked!

Bobby remained in the custody of her parents. After spending several months in jail, Sarah wrote me about the trial. Her parents didn't want us to know about it, fearing that we would try to gain custody of Bobby. Sarah also wrote that when Bob went back to "help," he had appeared with a gun. He claimed he was going to get whoever really killed the baby. This was during a period when there were many hijackings. There was a lot of publicity about the thorough searching of air travelers. Perhaps that is why Bob suggested taking a bus to New York. Sarah was as untruthful as Bob, so we will never really know what did happen.

Months later Bob appeared at the door with all his belongings in a knapsack. He was dirty, exhausted, and hungry. We weakened. "Okay, you can have the couch in the den, but only until you get a job. We won't help you with a car this time. You can use one of our bicycles to get to work and back."

"That's okay, Mom," he answered. "I'm really going to get my head on straight this time, I promise."

His promises held nothing for me anymore. A neighboring filling station needed trainees. Bob applied for the job after he got cleaned up. As usual his charm won him a job. He took the bicycle to work each afternoon and returned late at night after his shift.

One morning Don reappeared after leaving for work. "For two mornings," he mused, "the same car has been sitting just around the corner from the house when I go to work. It isn't there when I come home, and I just wonder if Bob has picked up a car someplace. Just because the bicycle is gone doesn't mean he's riding it. I have a feeling about that car. I'm going to come home today about the time he leaves for work to check it out."

"Lying again? I hope not," was all I could say.

When Don came home, Bob was busy putting the bicycle into the car and preparing to leave. "Where did you get the car?" Don asked.

"It belongs to a kid who works with me, and I'm buying it."

"Why have you been untruthful about the bicycle? Why not tell us you're buying a car? Will you never learn that it's best to be truthful?"

"What difference does it make? I haven't asked you for any money to pay for it. This friend trusts me until payday. I will pay him so much each time I get paid. It only cost a hundred bucks."

It wasn't worth the price, but Don felt the car was in such bad condition that Bob was probably being truthful. If he had stolen it, he'd have picked a better one. "We'll talk about it tomorrow," Don said, then went back to the house.

The next morning Bob was nowhere to be found. Shortly after four in the afternoon the telephone rang. Donny was at home. "Is Bob there?" a man asked.

"No, may I ask who is calling?" Donny questioned.

"This is his boss. He was to report to work at three. Does he want his job?"

"I don't know," Donny answered.

At that time we were living in an apartment while building a house. Bob had been home such a short time that he was unaware of the new house's location. We decided that the only way to keep him from continually appearing on the doorstep was to prevent him from knowing where we lived. We would then be saved the heartbreak of turning him away. A week before we were to move, the doorbell rang. I answered the door and met a plainclothed police officer holding out his badge. My heart hit my toes.

"What can I do for you? I asked.

"Mrs. Nyberg?"

I nodded. "Yes."

"Is Bob at home?"

"No, he doesn't live here, and we don't know where he is at present."

"May I come in and look around?" he asked.

Don came into the room and inquired who the man was.

The police officer again showed his identification. "Come in," Don said. "We have nothing to hide, and we certainly wouldn't hide our son from the authorities."

"Why are you looking for him?" I asked.

He looked up at me and said one word, "Rape."

What next? We each knew what the other was thinking. As the officer went from room to room, I questioned him further. "How old a girl is he accused of raping?"

"I don't know her age, but she isn't a minor. Her husband is pressing charges."

This fact relieved my mind somewhat. Any rape charge is terrible, but if the woman were married, it could mean she and Bob had been caught by her husband and she hollered "rape" to protect herself.

The officer continued his search, even looking in the shower stall. Don said afterward that he felt like asking the officer why he didn't look under the beds. The officer finally left, leaving his card and telling us to call him if we heard from Bob. He further explained, "Bob was arrested and released on his own recognizance, and then he failed to appear in court. So the judge isued a warrant for his arrest." We assured him we would let him know if we heard from Bob.

Soon our move into the new house was completed. This time Bob would not know where to find us. He knew where Don's office was and he had the office telephone number. He was also aware he could find us every Sunday morning at the 9:00 service at our church.

During the months when we didn't know Bob's whereabouts, my emotions were mixed. I felt relief because we were beyond the circumference of his temper, dishonesty, and con man activities, but I also felt guilty for being relieved. When he was out of our lives, it was so much easier to leave him totally in God's hands. But each time that Bob came home I seemed to take him back from God. I knew I had to let the guilt dissolve. I knew God was in command whether we were in contact with Bob or not.

During this period my father became seriously ill. Bob

telephoned one evening when Don was working late. He told Bob that his grandfather was gravely ill. Bob promised to keep in touch. He wouldn't tell us where he was, however, except to say he was "into horses" and working at a stable. That is where the police officer had told us Bob had been living, so we had nothing new to report as to his whereabouts.

Several months later Bob called to report that the police had picked him up on the rape charge, but that it had all been a mistake. He was found not guilty, so we didn't have to worry about reporting on him. Could he come home again? Would we tell him where we lived? The answer we continued to give was no.

Don had moved his office into our new home, so when the business phone rang at night we were sure it was Bob. Each time he'd ask where we were living, and we'd counter by asking him where *he* was living. He didn't want to answer so he would drop the question.

One night as I was preparing supper, the phone rang. It was my dad, recently out of the hospital and confined to a wheelchair. "Dorothea," he whispered, "I think your mother has had a stroke."

"Oh, Dad," I exclaimed, "are you all right? Have you called the doctor?"

"Yes," he said.

"I'll be right there." Donny and Don were just coming into the house for dinner. I was telling them about the call when we heard the office phone ring. Don and I ran out to the car while Donny went to answer the business phone. It was Bob. "What's new?" he casually asked. Donny told him what had happened, and Bob promised to call back the next day to see how they both were. He never called.

Dad suffered a massive heart attack while Mom was in the hospital. Just like when Grandfather Nyberg had died two years earlier, we had no idea where Bob was living. The rest of the family had flown east for Grandpa Nyberg's funeral without Bob. Now Bob would miss my Dad's funeral too.

My grief was so heavy that without Jesus I am certain I

would have reached the breaking point. Bob's seeming inability to care for anyone but himself was a sign of instability. Since there was no help available from medical or psychiatric sources, our only choice was to rely more heavily on the Lord.

Despite our new resolve to relinquish Bob to God, we were all shattered. Perhaps it was because both grandfathers had loved him unconditionally. *Why can't he learn to love?*

17
Horses, Horses

It was five more months before we heard from Bob again. He still did not know where we lived, so he used the one sure way of locating us—he came to church. With him was a young girl he introduced as Betty. She appeared to be about twelve or thirteen. Bob whispered to me in an undertone, "Don't mention Sarah or Bobby!"

We talked together in front of the church before going inside and being ushered to our seats. I told Bob about Dad's death, and he made no comment. Once we were seated, he continued to whisper questions until the service started. "Will you tell me where you live now?"

"Will you tell me where you live?" I countered.

"No," he replied.

"Well, two can play at that game. When we know for sure that you have your head on straight, as you put it, there will be time enough to tell." He gave me a dirty look and sat quietly through the service. Afterwards we invited them to go to breakfast with us.

"Betty is one of my students," Bob stated. "I teach riding at a stable. Why don't you guys come to a horse show sometime and watch?"

"If you tell us when one is going to be held, maybe we can make it."

I talked quietly to him while Don was visiting with Betty. "How old is this child?"

"Oh, Mom, I don't know," he answered evasively.

"You be careful. She's obviously a minor and dotes on you. It shows."

"She's just a student of mine."

"Okay, but be careful. I have to warn you."

"Her mom and dad have been so nice to me. They really like me and have been more like parents to me than you have. We usually go to their church on Sunday."

"I'm delighted that you have found someone you can relate to, Bob."

We parted ways after breakfast and returned home wondering about his young friend and her family. Several weeks later Bob telephoned. "Mom, I wanted you to know I'm staying at Betty's house. Her dad had a heart attack, and her mom doesn't want Betty to be alone at night while she is at the hospital. I just wanted you to know, and I'll give you the telephone number in case you want me."

A few more weeks passed, and Bob called again. "Mom, I need my birth certificate. Will you bring it to the horse show Saturday?" He gave me directions, and Mother rode with me to the stables to deliver the requested certificate. I went to the announcing booth and had him paged. He walked to the car with me to see his grandmother. She hadn't seen Bob for months and, of course, not since Dad had died. Bob was very sweet to her, telling her how nice she looked and making pleasant small talk. Suddenly he announced, "I gotta go or I'll miss the next event." With a wave he trotted off. He was still being true to form; we saw him only when he needed something from us—even something as minute as a birth certificate.

About a month later I received a letter that gave us a great deal to contemplate. It was from Betty's mother, telling us what a wonderful son we had. She told of the help Bob had been during her husband's illness and how the fact that Bob had been able to say such beautiful prayers at mealtime had been such a strength to her. She simply glowed in her reference to our son.

It was magnificent to hear, but we felt he had told her we would have nothing to do with him. She seemed to be trying to be a go-between in bringing Bob back into our family circle. She closed the letter by stating that Bob did not know she was writing to us.

The very same day the letter arrived, Bob telephoned. "I'm taking Betty south to a horse show. Her parents can't go because of her father's health."

I didn't comment about his traveling unchaperoned with such a young girl, but we went to bed with a prayer for knowledge as to how to handle the situation. Bob obviously had completely changed or had fooled the family. The letter Betty's mother had written showed she was unaware of his past history. We feared she might not have been as willing to send her daughter off with him had she known. What could we do?

In the morning I sat down and composed a letter:

My husband and I were so pleased to receive your lovely letter. It does a mother's heart good to hear such a glowing report of her son. This is a side of Bob we have seldom seen. I have heard this type of report repeatedly about our other sons, and we can't tell you how happy we are to hear of Bob's attitude toward your family. I believe it proves the proverb, "Train up a child in the way he should go, and when he is old, he will not depart from it" (Proverbs 22:6).

We turned Bob over to the Lord many years ago, because it was the only way we could go. We are delighted to hear he is finally growing up.

I attempted to make the letter show we had had problems with Bob without saying so in exact words. We wanted Betty's parents to be aware that their daughter should, perhaps, not be sent off alone with Bob.

A few days later Bob telephoned to say he had returned early from the horse show. "Can I come home again? I'm quitting the horse racket."

Again we told him, "Sorry, but no."

An interesting follow-up to Bob's stay with Betty and her family occurred several years later. Betty's mother telephoned and invited me to have lunch with her. She was curious about what Bob was doing. I met her, and we had an interesting conversation.

"Bob was really Betty's first love," she told me. "There must have been over ten years' difference in ages. But as I look back, it was a healthy experience for her."

I didn't ask too many questions because I felt I would rather not have some of the answers. She continued, "Betty is also an adopted child. She was at a stage of mixed emotions about her biological parents. Bob helped her with that when he told her, 'Betty, I found my real parents and they were nothing but a couple of drunks. You're better off forgetting you ever had any other parents.' Betty took his advice and told us she wasn't interested in who they were anymore."

"That's amusing," I replied, "because I know Bob has never seen his biological parents. He has told me he has absolutely no desire to try to find them because they gave him away."

"That surprises me, but Bob helped in other ways," Betty's mother continued. "He could say such nice table blessings. We always took turns saying grace. It was Betty's turn one particular meal, and she said one of the short, rote prayers we all learned as children. When she finished, Bob said to her, 'My mom always told us to pray from our hearts. You can say your own prayers, Betty; you don't need to recite those kid prayers.' It was a beautiful lesson and one that accomplished something because it didn't come from me."

"It is exciting to hear how much of what we taught Bob came through when we wanted to use it," I answered. "It really does prove that proverb I quoted in my letter to you several years ago about training up a child. This has been a delightful visit. Parents of kids who have strayed from their teachings need this kind of encouragement. I'm so glad you called me. God does work in wondrous ways," I shared as we parted.

"Don," I said that evening as I recalled my visit with Betty's mother, "it was a great afternoon. Betty's mother shared so many nice things about Bob that I really feel encouraged to praise God for him. It's amazing how much God has allowed Bob to absorb—more than I dreamed. He *can* use his training when he wants to—he really hasn't rebelled against everything!"

The next time Bob surfaced, he was working as a mechanic. He began calling us again to ask for money. "I'm fixing up an old car for my new girl friend. Linda and I are living in a motel. I haven't got a job, and we need money. The work at the garage got slow, so they laid me off."

"You'd better find work or try Linda's family for a handout. We're through doling out funds to you."

"They won't help," Bob stated. "Her mom's dead, and her dad doesn't like her. He won't help; he even took her horse away from her."

"Perhaps it was because she moved in with you. That's not too unreasonable for a parent to do, Bob. Some of us are a bit old-fashioned and don't buy this 'shacking up' arrangement."

A few months later he called again. "We're assistant managers of a motel and doing just great. Will you and Dad come for dessert tommorow night and meet Linda?"

We went, but we were not too favorably impressed with Linda. While we were there, Bob received a call about an outside light being out. Don went with him to replace the bulb. Bob couldn't locate the necessary bulb so he nonchalantly shrugged his shoulders and said, "Forget it. The day guy can do it."

We figured this job wouldn't last long, and it didn't. Next we heard, "We're assistant managers of a nice apartment complex near where you used to live. We get a two-bedroom apartment, but we need furniture. Have you got anything we could use?"

This move was an improvement in neighborhood over their previous motel job. *Perhaps,* we thought, *it's now the time to allow Bob to know where we live.* We invited them to come to the house and get some odds and ends of furniture. From then on they popped in and out all the time.

Linda started calling me "Mom." My mother became "Gram." This was not especially to our liking, but we made no comment. She was very anxious for Bob to get his divorce so they could be married. We weren't too sure that would be a good idea. We didn't agree with their living arrangement, but we also felt they would not have a stable marriage.

After about three months at the new apartment complex they were fired again. They gave us a mixture of stories as to why, but none of them placed any blame on themselves. They wanted funds or the chance to stay with us. The answer remained no.

From the apartment they moved into a commune-style setup with a group of Linda's friends. We heard nothing from them for a long period of time. Then they started stopping by at mealtime. Bob was looking for work, but Linda had a job as a telephone solicitor selling air conditioners.

Their lives seemed fairly stable at this point. Bob never remained out of work for long. Something always came along. We continued to put Bob in the Lord's hands. We could do nothing for him, and we knew God would have to win the battles that lay ahead.

18
Incarceration

Bob's communal living led to a deeper pitfall. He acquired a job as a security guard and approached us for money. "But Mom," he asked, "I can't get the job unless I have sixty-nine bucks for uniforms. I can start tonight if you'll lend it to me."

Once again we acquiesed. We didn't like to see him doing this type of work, but we were trying to let him run his own life. It was, as usual, to be a short-term loan.

Each time he'd call, I'd ask how soon I would receive a payment on the uniform loan. "Next payday," he'd always reply. Finally, for lack of an excuse, he quit calling or coming over. He had received a promotion and now had armed patrol duty with a license to carry a gun.

One day Donny's wife, Cheryl, and I were chatting in the kitchen. Fresh-from-the-oven cookies filled the room with a tantalizing aroma that said "Eat me!" I had just put the last sheet of cookies in the oven when the phone rang. It was Linda.

"Mom, Bob is in jail. He's been there for a week. Will you bail him out?"

"No!"

"But," she added, "the jail is terrible. I'll pay you back so much a week. I'm making good money at my job."

"What's he in jail for?"

"They claim he robbed a store, but he couldn't have. He

was with me when it happened. Somebody used his car. The police traced the license number to Bob."

Cheryl's face was crestfallen as she listened. Quietly she slipped upstairs as I replaced the receiver in the cradle. I don't know how long I stood in silence, tears running down my face.

After a while Cheryl handed me a slip of paper, gave me a gentle hug, and left. I looked down and read:

Dear Mother,

I wish I could tell you this face to face, but I know I would cry. So . . . I don't have the answer to the new problem with Bob, but I have a prayer that I would like to pray to and for you.

Dear Father,

We come to you—our hearts filled with sorrow. Bob , one of your children, is doing wrong. You know all the problems. We don't know where to turn but to you. Father, Dorothea needs all your strength to handle it. They put Bob in your hands as a baby. He is your child. We don't know how this had happened, but give us the faith to handle it. Keep your hand on her shoulder, guide her in your direction. We know you can and will. We rerelease Bob to you. Amen.

Mom, I don't know if these are the right words, but it's what came to me. You're the best Mom and have the best things:
1. A wonderful husband
2. A wonderful mother who, I know, still holds your name in her prayers daily.
3. Wonderful sons
4. And best of all—the best—Jesus Christ!

I love you, we all love you.

Strengthened by this lovely encouragement, I telephoned Don. We agreed to ask an attorney friend, Hank Anderson, to handle bail. This was a new experience for our family. Hank offered to go to the jail, see Bob, and find out what happened. When Hank came back he reported, "If you can see your way clear to getting him out, I'd advise it. Bob is pretty scared and is in with some tough guys. Apparently he didn't do the robbery, but he was driving the car. He was in a neighboring store buying something when a kid who lives with them took his gun and pulled the robbery. Bob drove away anyway. It was a stupid thing to do, and Bob realizes it now. He's really frightened. It's a confused story."

"His stories usually are!" I replied.

Don and I talked it over and decided once again to give in to his request for money. We put up the nonrefundable two hundred and fifty dollar bond, plus security for the balance. We decided against supplying the entire cost. If we had put up the entire two thousand five hundred dollars, we would have received it all back when Bob's trial was completed, but if he jumped bail or failed to appear, we would have to forfeit the entire amount. We figured it better to gamble on never being repaid the two hundred and fifty dollars.

Bob was out on bail approximately three months while awaiting trial. Then a judge sentenced him to one year in jail. Sadly, he now has a felony on his record for the rest of his life. It was a costly mistake. The youngster who did the actual robbery was a minor and got off with a scolding. Bob spent his time behind bars, a sobering experience. While in jail he wrote:

Dear Mother and Father
Well I stil have not seen or herd from Linda Well I hope you will cal and find out what hapen to her I hope she is allright You no this has done me a lot of good in ways ive been doing a lot of thinkin this few months Ive been loked up I no if I had to do it over my life it wood be change I dont have any were to go wen I get out Find where my car is ok call the wemem jail and see if Linda is in jail ok After I get out Im going to stay way from girls and get my life straiton out My PO is out to get me it sem like he wants to give me 9 mor month Love your son Bob

Again a family friend came to the rescue, offering a factory job to Bob if he were eligible for a work-release program. The details were worked out with his probation officer. Bob was allowed to leave jail every morning with a packed lunch, and he reported back by a specific time each evening. His salary was sent to the county. They kept a certain amount for room and board, while he was given transportation money and a small amount for clothing and spending. The rest was held until his release.

Linda had written some bad checks as Linda Nyberg. Bob was liable for their repayment. This, too, was deducted from his pay. During this time Linda took Bob's car and disappeared. We later discovered that her job was not telephone soliciting; it was plain and simple soliciting. . . .

19
New Life, New Wife

As Bob's jail term drew to a close, we began to ask the question that faced us through the years: What next? Bob was due to be released in two weeks *if* he had a place to stay. He wrote and asked if he could please come home. We replied that we would take him in until he found an apartment. Young people from the college age fellowship at church had been going to visit him. From within this group he had made some friends. We hoped they would stand by him.

We picked him up from work on the day he was released. He was esctatic to be free, and we spent an enjoyable week apartment-hunting while he got used to coming and going without restrictions. He took one of the girls from church out one evening, and they had a delightful time. We hoped this friendship would continue. She was strong in spirit, would be good for him, and might keep him active in the group's activities.

Bob located an apartment and went about setting up housekeeping. He enjoyed independent living again. The college group planned a weekend retreat and, although he didn't have the funds to pay his way, it was arranged for him to go through a "campership." He had bought a car and was going to drive, but he didn't show up at the appointed place, and the group left without him.

When I found out he had let the group down, I telephoned him and asked what happened. "Oh, something else came up," he replied. We feared he was returning to his old, undependable ways.

The following weekend Bob appeared at our home with a new girl and a different car. "Where did you get that car?" I asked.

"It's Jane's. Mom, I want you to meet Jane."

"Hi," I said, not being too friendly. *Where did she come from?* I wondered. Soon they were off. "Where does he find new friends in such a short time?" I quizzed Don.

"It's that charm! It never fails him, I guess."

The next time I talked to Bob, I asked, "Truthfully, now, Bob, where did you meet Jane?"

"Oh, I started writing to her while I was in jail."

"How did you get her name to write to her? She isn't from this neighborhood, I gather."

"No, she lives in the valley and is going to college."

"How did you find her?" I repeated my question.

"Well, her girlfriend's boyfriend was in jail with me."

This grieved me. We were hoping Bob would stick with the young people from church. Soon it became evident that Jane was spending weekends with Bob. She lived almost fifty miles away, and they were together every Saturday and Sunday. We knew it was too far for her to be driving back and forth. When Bob went to see her, he didn't drive back and forth, either. We presumed they were living together weekends.

One day Bob reported, "Jane's mother and stepfather want us to get married this summer."

"Bob, you aren't divorced yet. How can you talk of marriage? Does Jane know about Sarah?"

"No, and don't you dare tell her."

"I won't tell her, but if she asks anything I would have to lie to answer, I won't do it. You must tell her."

"Why should I? She'll only be hurt."

"Yes, but she's going to be hurt anyway. She has evidently trusted you and thought you were free to marry. You simply have to tell her. Where are they planning to hold the wedding —in a church?"

"Yes, in the Catholic church. I told them I would not become a Catholic but I'd be married there."

"You can't be married in the Catholic church if you're divorced, and she can't marry a divorced man and remain an active Catholic. You cannot hide this fact. You have a son, one who looks exactly like you and who has an identical name. Someday he may want to find you. How will Jane feel when a young man knocks at the door and says that he is your son."

"That couldn't ever happen."

"Oh yes it could! Sarah could decide to find you, too. But most important, this is no way to start a marriage—with a lie. Honesty is a most important ingredient in a marriage. For once, Bob, tell the truth! Tell Jane about Sarah and Bobby."

The next time we heard from Bob, he and a young man from work had moved to a larger apartment. It soon became apparent that Jane was living there, too.

It surprised us that, with her intelligence, Jane would move into this kind of situation. However, we kept our thoughts to ourselves and waited. Jane's father was deceased, and she was receiving Social Security payments while she was in school. This was a help to their finances, because Bob's salary couldn't support them both.

Jane telephoned one day. "I want to thank you for making Bob tell me about his marriage. It was a terrible shock. I couldn't believe he would lie to me about anything so serious. I told him that I still love him, but it hurt me deeply."

"I'm so thankful he finally told you," I said. "He couldn't expect or shouldn't want to keep anything as important as that from you. I, too, am glad and appreciate your telling me he has fulfilled that obligation."

We received a letter from Sarah some months later. I didn't know what her incarceration status was, but she wanted Bob to know she had obtained a divorce. She didn't know how to reach Bob. I gave her letter to Bob, and he said, "I'll give it to my lawyer. He's working on the divorce." We didn't know he had an attorney.

Two weeks later the friend who hired Bob met me on the street and said, "Congratulations on your new daughter-in-law." Apparently I looked shocked, because he added, "Didn't you know the kids got married?"

"No, we didn't. But aren't the parents often the last to know?" I laughed.

"Well, as long as I started the story, I might as well finish it. Bob asked for a few days off, and he and Jane went to Vegas and got married. She's had a diamond for a long time."

"Apparently she took it off when they were with us. I hope he's certain his divorce is final. I'm glad, I guess, that they have made their arrangement legal."

Later that evening I told Don of my conversation with Bob's boss. "Maybe, just maybe, this is the answer to our prayer. Jane is a lady, a lovely young girl. Maybe she will be able to keep Bob on the straight and narrow. She loves him unconditionally, and that's what he needs. She willingly gave up her Social Security payments by getting married, and that's another plus. To legalize their situation was more important to her than the easy money."

As time went on, Bob and Jane really became an integral part of our family. Our holiday celebrations were once again complete family gatherings. It was a pleasant change after so many holidays of wondering where Bob was and what he was doing.

Our son David, his wife, Judy, and their small daughter, Susie, came for a vacation. Judy had never met Bob. We didn't even know where Bob was at the time of their wedding. Since Dave and Judy lived in northern California, there had been no other opportunity for her to meet Bob. They both had reservations about the get-together, but little Susie with the honesty of a baby ran to Bob and threw herself into his arms. Bob always had a way with small children, and his niece was no exception. Her enthusiasm for her new uncle and aunt thrilled me.

A few months later Mom suffered another severe stroke. Jane was a lifesaver to me. She came and sat with Mom when I had to get away for something. Truly a wonderful addition to the Nyberg clan, Jane was the balance of quiet to Bob's boisterousness, a calming influence on his overenthusiasm. She was a fine housekeeper and cook, and she continued in her courses at college. She worked part-time to help with expenses and was totally giving of herself. In short, we fell in love with our daughter-in-law.

I apologized to her one day about my attitude toward her the first time we met. "That's okay, Mom," she replied with a laugh. "I expected a cool reception from all the tales Bob told about the family. I know now that they aren't true, but at the time it was what I expected. Bob has a problem, I know, but I'm not perfect either, and I love him."

Jane's words uplifted me, and later that afternoon I prayed. *God, you're so good! Your plan is always perfect. Is Bob one of those people who just take longer to fit in with your design? I know he's not fully in step yet, but he seems nearer than before. I know you are with him, whether he knows it or not.*

It seemed to me that Bob was finally on the road to renewal. I didn't expect any devastating detours.

20
Repeat Performance

Early Monday morning as I laid my Bible aside, I was startled by the jangle of the phone bell. Jane's voice greeted me when I picked up the receiver.

"Mom, I've left Bob." Her voice was barely audible. "I can't tell you how hard it is for me to do this or how I hate to tell you, but I just can't take any more. He lies to me all the time."

"Do you want to tell me what happened?" I answered softly. "You don't need to. When he lost his job a few weeks ago, Dad and I prayed this wouldn't be too much, added to what you've already been through with him. We were relieved when he found another job so soon. We both felt that if you walked out, he might disappear again."

"Yes, I know, and I still love him, but he's smashing my self-esteem bit by bit. He told me he had to work Saturday. When he dressed in good clothes, I wondered if he was really going to work. I asked a neighbor to drive me to the factory. It was closed, the parking lot empty, and the gate locked.

"He came home that evening," she continued, "complained about how tired he was, and fell into bed exhausted. He told me he had to work Sunday, too. I said nothing because I didn't want to make him mad, and I was ashamed for checking up on him . . . but I had to. When he left for work, I waited awhile, packed my belongings, and went to my parent's home. I haven't heard from him." Her voice quivered. "I h-have to hang up n-now." By this time she was sobbing.

The phone clicked. I mechanically replaced the receiver. My stomach churned. No bright victory, no miraculous change, no "happily ever after" for this young couple. Somewhere along the road I failed to see the sign, "Caution: Watch for Falling Rocks!"

I buried my head in my arms. "Help me, Lord. You have been patient with me as I've tried to learn to relinquish this son to you. He is yours, you're in charge! And please, Lord, help Jane survive."

Like most families, ours has known happiness and despair, I'm convinced God put Bob into our lives for a purpose—to teach us to wait quietly in his presence for the next step. Whatever caused Bob's behavior problems—psychopathic personality, dyslexia, heredity—the only solution is death to himself and rebirth in Jesus Christ. We cannot hurry that process.

As I sat thinking about my errant son, a memory surfaced. A young chaplain's wife who worked at County Juvenile Hall had spoken to our women's group at church and told some of her experiences in the detention home.

"I speak their language," she explained. "When they gripe about their backgrounds, I tell them I can match anything they've experienced and go them one better. My mother was a psychopathic personality, and my life was hell! My mom found the Lord before she died, though, and that made everything I went through worthwhile."

After the meeting I talked with her and shared a bit about Bob. At the time we didn't know his whereabouts.

"Mrs. Nyberg," she said, "pray he will meet someone who can lead him in the right path. You can't reach him, but someone can. Just keep prayer wafting heavenward. Never give up!"

Recalling this conversation, my prayer that morning again became one of relinquishing Bob and his problems to the Lord.

Later Bob called to report, "Mom, I came home and found Jane gone . . . and most of our stuff, too. I called her parents.

Her dad answered and told me Jane had been sent away and that I'd hear from their attorney. What should I do?"

What should he do? What should he have done long ago? Why couldn't this manchild get his priorities in order?

I told Bob I had no answers for him. Then I called Jane's parents and asked to speak to Jane. "Jane is to have no contact whatever with anyone in the Nyberg family. Bob is being served divorce papers and that is all we have to say to you!" was the response.

"Please tell Jane," I replied, "that we feel she made the correct decision, that we love her, and that we always will."

In reply I heard a "Hrruummph" and the crash of the receiver.

Bob disappeared again. Several weeks later he reappeared to introduce us to a new girlfriend with whom he was living in her parent's home.

Bob began to call from time to time to ask for money or to move home again. Each time we firmly answered no.

During this period my mother passed away. Once again Bob was the only member of our family who did not attend the memorial service.

Then one evening Bob called. "Just wanted to say hi and see if everyone is okay."

We had a pleasant chat with no requests for anything. He closed with the statement that he was tired and going to get to bed early.

Later that evening when Don and I were in the first throes of a deep sleep, the phone rang. "This is City Hospital," the voice said. I was instantly wide awake. "Is this the Nyberg residence?"

"Yes."

"Your son Bob has just been brought into the emergency room. He has a badly mangled leg and wants you to come to the hospital."

"We'll be right there." I gasped.

We dressed and drove to the hospital where we met an orthopedic surgeon. "Come in and let me show you the X-rays.

The femur is broken," he explained. "We'll put him in traction to pull the bone back together. The lower leg is the big problem. It's a compound fracture and will take hours of surgery to clean out the pieces of dead bone and try to patch it all together."

"Can it be done?" We both asked when we saw the shattered bone in the X-ray. "Can you really save his leg?"

"I'll do it! But it will take a long time. There's no need for you to sit around here. Go home to bed. I'll call you when I'm through." He smiled. "It isn't necessary for all of us to lose a night's sleep."

We saw Bob just before we left the hospital. He was sedated but still in pain. His leg was bloody and seemingly bent in all directions. We questioned the possibility of its being saved.

"Hang in there, Bob," Don said as he squeezed his hand. "The doctor told us to go home. He'll call us when you're out of surgery."

"We'll be praying for you and the surgeon," we reassured him as the nurses readied him for surgery.

Hours later the call came. "It was worse than I anticipated, but we've saved the leg!"

"Thank you, God," we prayed.

Each time we visited Bob, a young nurse's aide named Sandy was hovering over him. One day he introduced us to her, saying she was "his special nurse."

I saw it coming . . . another conquest, another girl bewitched by our con man, and the charm that never failed.

Adoration shone from Sandy's eyes as she acknowledged the introduction. *What is it,* I silently questioned, *that attracts so many girls to this mixed-up young man? Why is his charm so forceful?*

When he was released from the hospital, he moved home to recuperate. Sandy visited him almost every evening. On her free days they went out together. One night as she was leaving, she asked, "How would you feel if I told you Bob and I wanted to be married?"

With no hesitation I replied, "I'd be sick!"

"Why?" she countered.

"Because he isn't ready for another commitment. His last divorce isn't final, he has no job, he isn't stable. I could go on and on with a zillion reasons."

"I know all about his past," she assured me. "He's told me everything. God has taught him a lesson through all this. He really has changed."

"Wait until he is out of the cast and free to come and go. Be certain he's changed before you jump into marriage. Don't be in a rush."

That old charm still worked! There was nothing more we could say. They were two consenting adults. As soon as his divorce from Jane was final, he and Sandy were married, his leg still in a cast.

During the next two years they presented us with two more grandchildren, constant requests for financial help, and frequent threats to leave each other. Theirs was a stormy marriage, and we wept for the two little ones awash in the center of their matrimonial storms.

Our merry-go-round never seemed to stop whirling. Bob was often in trouble, so calls came repeatedly for bail money and attorney's fees. They were evicted from apartments and had no place to live. They had no diapers for the children. On and on came the demands. Tough love was our motto. We tried to say no but at times weakened for the sake of our grandchildren.

For years Bob had talked about finding his brothers and sister. Each time Don and I traveled to the state where we were all born, Bob asked us to look for them.

Don is quiet, but when he speaks, I listen. "If Bob wants to find his family, he must do it himself. He's an adult, and it's his responsibility. We can help, but he must do the footwork."

As usual Don was right. We gave Bob copies of his adoption papers. He took Sandy and the children to the county of his birth and discovered he was part of a family of nine children.

He called to report, "Mom, I met one of my brothers today. When he rang the doorbell, I opened the door to see my double standing there. It was kinda teary."

"Kinda?" I replied. "It must have been very teary!"

"Yeah, I guess so." Then he casually added, "I may try to get my real birth certificate."

Knowing well how Bob's mind works, I felt certain he was thinking of changing his name to the name on his original birth certificate. I wanted to give him our blessing—the final step in this mother's journey to total relinquishment.

Late that evening I sat at my typewriter and wrote and rewrote from the depths of my heart a letter I felt drawn to write.

In the morning I shared it with Don. Then with his approval I took that final step of giving Bob up and with a hollow feeling posted the letter that day. I wrote:

Dear Bob,

Since your phone call last night my mind has swirled with memories. I pray that the right words will appear here and say what I really mean. These thoughts are from Dad's and my heart. . . . We love you, always have, and always will!

Yet even at the time of your first period of serious rebelliousness against our lifestyle, I wondered if you had been placed in the wrong home for your happiness. Our vacations were trips to cities in which we stayed in motels or with friends, visited points of interest, model homes, and such. You wanted to camp in a tent in the woods, fish, and do outdoorsy things. We sent you to camp every summer, which you loved, but the family activities bored you. You were the one who had to try to fit into our mold. David and Donny liked the things Dad and I do. You were the one who had to adapt or complain.

All these memories surface because you spoke about filling out papers to get your original birth certificate. Is this a step toward changing your name back to your birth name? If it is, we give you our blessing!

Years ago when you became a Nyberg, I was unaware of the strength in a person's genes. Genes affect our likes, dislikes, and personalities as well as coloring, stature, and facial features.

You told me how much your blood brothers look like you, how well you get along with them, and how you even think alike.

Your two youngsters are half you, half Sandy. They will grow to develop much the same personalities as the two of you. Their genes are your genes. That's one reason we give our blessing to changing your family's name. Maybe the new name will help your children grow up happily.

I'm writing this letter because I felt changing your name was part of your thoughts, and you might feel hesitant about doing it for fear of hurting us.

When we boarded babies those many years ago, we did it to try to make you understand that we loved those babies because we love children. Jesus said the most important rule to follow is to love one another. We may not all enjoy the same activities, food, type of clothes, or whatever, but *we must learn to love one another!*

We do love you, Bob. We are extremely happy you've found your birth family and enjoy their company. Dave and Donny think alike and feel alike and are alike because they are blood brothers. Naturally, you feel and look like your blood brothers, and this is no reflection on them or your adoptive brothers. It's just the way the world was made.

I'm certain God did not plan divorce, child neglect, or abuse, but it all started in the Garden of Eden when Adam and Eve couldn't leave the forbidden fruit alone. . . . and things have become progressively worse ever since.

Do what will make you most comfortable, Bob. You will be our son, whatever your name. Your birth Mom will, no doubt, be pleased to know you want to be a part of your birth family again. We'll love you either way. All we've ever wanted is your happiness.

My remaining and constant prayer is that you will get back to the biblical training you had in our home and turn your life over to Jesus. Then, perhaps, you can lead the rest of your clan to the Lord. That's the only way to live . . . for Jesus!

All our love,
Mom and Dad.